A PHOTOGRAPHIC AND LITERARY RECORD OF ULSTER LIFE

1880~1915

First published December 1974
Second impression December 1974

FACES OF THE PAST

BY
BRIAN MERCER WALKER

A PHOTOGRAPHIC AND LITERARY RECORD OF ULSTER LIFE

1880~1915

The Appletree Press Ltd
6 Dublin Road Belfast BT2 7HL

Dedicated to my mother and father

First published 1974 by
The Appletree Press Limited
6 Dublin Road, Belfast BT2 7HL.

Designed by
Spring Graphics Co.

Printed by
The Appletree Press Ltd,
4 Marcus Ward Street, Belfast BT7 1AP.

Hardback ISBN 0 904651 00 2
Paperback ISBN 0 904651 01 0

CONTENTS

PREFACE

I am very grateful to the many people who have helped me write this book. In particular I am much indebted to those friends who gave me continual encouragement during the time I was writing it especially Mary Punch, Patrick and Elizabeth Roche, William Vaughan, John and Yvonne Healey, Douglas Perrin and David and Felicity Haire. I also wish to thank for their generous help, Terence McCaughey, Olive Baskin, Christopher Woods, Jack Johnston, Jim Gracey, Sam Hanna Bell and Mrs. W. G. Kirkpatrick.

My work was greatly assisted by information and good advice from Bill Crawford, Brian Hutton and the staff of the Public Record Office of Northern Ireland, Brian Turner, Noel Nesbit and the staff of the Ulster Museum, Brendan Adams, Aiken McClelland and the staff of the Ulster Folk Museum, and James Vitty, Paula Howard and the staff of the Linenhall Library. Gratitude for their assistance must also be expressed to the staffs of the National Library of Ireland, the Royal Irish Academy, the British Museum, Queen's University Library, the Belfast Central Library and Armagh Museum.

My thanks are especially due to Merv and Pen Jones for their excellent work in designing the book and to the publisher for his invariable patience and efficiency. For their help in the production of the book I am grateful to J.P. McAlinden, S. Campbell, E. Kydd, P. McAvoy, P. Boyd and D.J.P. Webster.

To those people and institutions who gave permission for their photographs and extracts to be used I am much indebted.

Finally thanks must be extended to the governors of the Linenhall Library and the trustees of the Esme Mitchell Trust, without whose generous support the book might not have been published.

INTRODUCTION

FACES OF THE PAST, for several reasons, is not a conventional type of history. In the first place, it adopts the unusual approach of looking at life in Ulster at the turn of the century through the work and lives of two different types of contemporary artist — the photographer and the writer. In the second place the selection of artists includes not only well known photographers like R. J. Welch and famous poets such as William Allingham but also local photo-graphers, poets, novelists and playwrights. Presented in an original manner, the material in the book seeks to illustrate life in the province at this time in a way which is both appealing and interesting as well as novel.

The historical background

The period illustrated in these pages runs from the early 1880s to around 1915 - a time which witnessed important changes and events in Ulster. On the political front it saw the advent of the Unionist and Nationalist parties, the riots of 1886 and 1907, the Belfast strike of 1907, the 1912-14 home-rule crises and the outbreak of the First World War. But important as these political occurrences were they were probably over-shadowed in most people's everyday lives by the social and economic changes taking place in the province.

By 1901 Belfast was a city of 349,180 people, compared with 87,062 in 1851, and still rapidly expanding. Her shipyards and ropeworks were among the largest of their kind in the world. Linen factories were to be found not only in Belfast but in large numbers throughout the north of Ireland. Communications were improving with the introduction of the motor car and electric tram. In the countryside great changes were taking place with the tenant farmers gradually coming into ownership of their land; also new mechanised methods of farming were being adopted. Thanks to the education acts of the early part of the nineteenth century illiteracy was now largely a thing of the past.

This scene of progress and improvement was of course only part of the whole picture. In many areas traditional patterns of working and living remained. With the tremendous economic growth went other more disturbing features. Conditions were frequently harsh in the factories, sanitation was very inadequate in much of the new housing and life for many with no social security must often have been desperate. In the countryside farm labourers gained little from the changes. Social inequality was a glaring feature of the period. Such was the world in which our artists lived.

The photographer

R. W. Welch, one of our photographers, in an adventurous pose - sitting on the rock known as the Grey Man's Path, Fair Head, Co. Antrim (Welch Collection, Ulster Museum)

For the photographer equipped with his recently acquired craft, some facets of this much contrasting scene could be recorded in a new and exciting way. This he did, not in a matter of fact way but often vividly in a manner that captured something of the feeling of life in these years. We can see this clearly for example in the stark scene of the two women labouring in the field at Glenshesk, in the superbly impressive picture of the S.S.s *Titanic* and *Olympic* in the shipyards, or in the simple, silent portrait of the Newcastle fishwives that tells so much of suffering and toil. These photographs effectively illustrate not only life at this time but also the very remarkable skill of the photographers.

By the 1880s photography was well established in the province. The Ulster Amateur Photographic Society was founded in 1885. According to the census reports there were 74 professional photographers in Ulster in 1881 and by 1911 the number had risen to 223. For the professional photographer his job could have a number of aspects. Primarily he would have been concerned with private portraits. Increasingly, however, as the century went on he supplied photographs for postcards and book illustrations. Then when in the early part of the twentieth century photographs could be reproduced in newspapers his work took on an added dimension.

Of the photographers included in the book the first who should be mentioned is Robert John Welch (1859-1936). Born in Strabane, Co. Tyrone, he came to Belfast in 1875 to train. Besides being official photographer to a number of firms like Harland and Wolff he spent much of his career travelling around the country recording its scenery, antiquities and the life of its people; many of these photographs were used as illustrations in books. The principal collection of his plate glass negatives is in the Ulster Museum, Belfast.

Our next two photographers were also connected with Strabane. J. A. Burrows, about whom little is known, ran a photographic business in the town from about 1901 to 1913 when it was bought by Herbert Frederick Thomas Cooper, Born in 1874 at Hammersmith, London, Cooper settled in Strabane and ran the business until his death in 1960. The Cooper Collection, which includes some of Burrow's work, has now been deposited in the Public Record Office of Northern Ireland by his son, Mr. H. D. H. Cooper. It is the largest single collection of photographs in Ireland, numbering over 200,000 plate glass negatives, few of which have been published in book form before. The collection is chiefly concerned with routine family, wedding and passport photographs but around 20,000 cover a wide range of events in Co.'s Tyrone and Donegal.

Another important photographer included is William Alfred Green (1870-1958). Of Co. Down stock, he was educated in Lisburn, County

On a more serious note, this photograph taken in the Clogher Valley, Co. Tyrone, at the beginning of the century, shows something of the poverty to be found in the Ulster countryside. (Rose Shaw Collection Ulster Folk Museum).

Antrim. He became an apprentice assistant to R. J. Welch and then went into business on his own. Green had a special interest in folk customs and agricultural practices and devoted much of his time recording these, especially in the Toome Bridge area of Co. Antrim. Most of his work was done between 1910 and 1930. His photographs are in the Ulster Folk Museum, Cultra, Co. Down. Also in the Ulster Folk Museum are the photographs of Rose Shaw, an amateur photographer, who photographed rural life in the Clogher Valley, Co. Tyrone, where she lived in the early part of this century.

After these photographers, all of whom had close connections with Ulster, mention must be made of Robert French (1841-1917). A Dubliner he was chiefly responsible for taking the photographs in the Lawrence Collection in the National Library of Ireland. William Mervyn Lawrence, the original owner of this collection, ran a photographic business in Dublin and he employed French to travel to every part of Ireland taking photographs for his picture postcard work. As well as being used for postcards these photographs were used for advertisements and book illustrations.

In addition to the work of these six photographers, material has come from other collections of photographs. The Sprott Collection in Portadown College, Portadown, Co. Armagh is a collection of lantern slides by various photographers depicting life in Portadown from about 1880 to 1940. Miscellaneous collections in the Linenhall Library the Royal Irish Academy, the Public Record Office of Northern Ireland and the Ulster Museum provided suitable photographs as did a number of private albums. Where possible, in these latter cases, the photographer has been identified and his name given along with the location of the photograph. Some of the dates of the photographs are uncertain, but nearly all lie between 1880 and 1915.

The writer

Just as the photographer with his precise, factual illustrations can tell us much about life at this time so also can the writer with his subjective, imaginative accounts. For example, the poetry of Patrick MacGill, a one time navvy, gives an insight into the harsh depersonalised life of the navvy in a way that a mass of statistics about canals and railways could not.

In Louis Walsh's play, *The Pope at killybuck,* we can see something of the humour and prejudice of the Northern countryside. Again in Sir Samuel Ferguson's poem, 'In Carey's Footsteps' we have the intensely felt reaction of an individual to political violence, a subject unfortunately not unfamiliar to us today. The attitudes and prejudices sometimes shown in these writers' works are often revealing.

A number of general points can be made about the selection of authors. All are imaginative writers who were either born and brought up in Ulster or who spent an important part of their lives there. The political, social and religious backgrounds of these people differed considerably as did the subjects they wrote about. All were influenced to some degree by their connection with Ulster and so these extracts from their work along with the notes on the authors give us an interesting insight into life in the province at this time with all its differing personal experiences.

Next it can be noted that the authors represent both a narrower and a wider selection of literary talent than is customary in most anthologies. Each author is connected with Ulster and nearly all these examples of their work were written between 1880 and 1915. But at the same time they include not only playwrights who wrote for the Abbey Theatre and the Ulster Literary Theatre but also several who wrote for amateur drama groups. Again there are famous poets like William Allingham and unknown local poets such as Thomas Given, a farmer from Cullybackey, Co. Antrim. Some wrote in Ulster Scots vernacular, some in Irish and some in Queen's English. Over thirty writers are included. Also there are examples of religious verse, folk song and political doggerel as well as extracts from literary and satirical magazines. All together the selection provides a valuable cross section of cultural activity during this period.

Standards differed considerably between these authors as the extracts clearly show. Some like Sir Samuel Ferguson and William Allingham wrote material of the highest quality which can have a strong impact even today. Others like Margaret Dobbs were effective in their local context. In the case of certain of the writers, however, it may seem to the present day reader that their work is of little literary value. But it should be remembered that this is what people at the time wrote and what they read. A novelist such as Rosa Mulholland attracts no attention today from the reader or critic but in her time her books were serialized in newspapers all over the country and she was undoubtedly influential in creating and reinforcing social and political attitudes. These extracts do give us some idea of the general literary taste of the period.

Finally

Finally comment must be passed on the arrangement of material in the book. It is neither simply a collection of photographs nor an anthology of Ulster writers, but an experiment to bring the two together. The association between image and text may at times seem tenuous. But it exists and it is left to the reader to discover it. In some cases the photographs are linked with the writers themselves, not the extracts. Although every county in Ulster is represented by writers and photographs some, because of the availability of material, are better represented than others.

Such then are the aims and methods of *Faces of the past.* It portrays people and conditions and contemporaries' personal expressions about them. It reflects something of the diverse social, political and cultural personality of Ulster at this time. Besides all this, it shows the very considerable artistic talent emanating from the province in these years, not only at a sophisticated level of thinking and creating but also at the local level in the countryside. The choice of photographs and extracts is of course the author's personal one but it is hoped that the material selected will give the reader an interesting and evocative record of life in Ulster at the turn of the century.

Haymaking, 1915 style (Cooper Collection, Public Record Office of Northern Ireland)

Workers leaving the Belfast shipyards, 1911. The Titanic can be seen in the background. (Welch Collection, Ulster Museum).

INGLIS BREAD
SWEETEST & BEST

CRUMLIN RD

83

Right: Linen bleach greens such as this one somewhere in Co. Antrim, were a common sight in Ulster. The linen was laid out in the fields and carefully turned to allow slow and even atmospheric bleaching to take place. (Lawrence Collection, National Library of Ireland).

Thomas Given, a farmer from Cullybackey, Co. Antrim, was one of three brother poets. As was the custom of many rural poets, he wrote for local newspapers. Also like many others he used the dialect of his own district. He does not seem to have been a weaver himself at any stage, but his use of various weaving terms in this poem suggests that he had a good knowledge of the trade. Given died in 1917 at the age of 67.

Below: A handloom damask weaver at Waringstown, Co. Down, around 1890. By this time independent weavers were few in number, the factories having usurped their position. (Sprott Collection, Portadown College)

THE WEAVER QUESTION

We read o' meetings to support
   The risin' nerra-gauge,
Which is to be the strength and fort
   O' every comin' age.
We read o' controversies lang,
   O' puirhoose jaw and vapour,
But seldom does the weavers' wrang
   Bedeck the public paper
         On ony day.

Oor wabs are lang an' ill to weave—
   Sometimes the yarn is bad—
Till scanty claes, wi' ragget sleeve,
   Is seen on lass an' lad.
But noo guid fortune we'll attain,
   For orators sae thrifty
Will gar the dreeper clip his chain
   Wa' doon tae twa-an'-fifty
         On ilka day.

Queels maun be wun when claith is wroucht,
   An' pickers, shears an' treadles,
Tallow an' temples maun be boucht,
   An' floor tae dress the heddles.
Then meat tae gar the wee yins leeve,
   Maun come as weel's the tackle,
But shure the wages we receive
   Wud hardly buy them treacle
         Tae meal this day.

How aisy 'tis for men tae preach
   Whun riches they hae got,
An' wae self-interest's purse-hurt screech,
   Ca' us a sinfu' lot.
But, haud a wee! ye men o' wealth!
   Though noo for breath yer pantin',
We ax nae favours gained by stealth—
   It's justice that we're wantin'—
         Nae mair this day.

I ne'er was blessed wae gift o' gab,
   Like some great learned men,
Instead o' school, I wove my wab,
   Before that I was ten.
Though noo I'm auld an' gray's my hair,
   I've studied weel the sense o't
For work let us get wages fair,
   Nae matter 'boot the length o't
         On ony day.

Thomas Given from G. R. Buick's *Poetical works of the brothers Given* (Belfast, 1900), pp 190-1.

HERE, approximately, are a few instances of the wages paid to women in the spinning and weaving mills of Belfast. Preparers, spreaders, drawers and rovers get from 8s. 6d. to 11s. per week; spinners earn from 11s. 6d. to 13s.; reelers from 15s. to 17s.; weavers and winders from 8s. to 14s.; though those who are engaged in fine weaving or damask work earn up to 18s. to 19s. As for male workers in these industries, skilled labourers like flax-dressers are paid from 24s. to 28s. per week, and roughers from 20s. to 24s.

These figures, however, give a rather flattering idea of the wages paid in the textile industries, for it must be remembered that it is always possible that either the cut-throat competition which continually goes on between the spinning and the weaving industries, or some other cause of trade depression, may result in the mills working only short time. Towards the end of 1907, for instance, all the spinning mills were working for half-time for nearly twelve months, and a friend of mine tells me of a reeler he knew, a married woman, who was trying during all that time to support a family on 6s. 3d. a week. Skilled male labourers, like flax-roughers, were for a time making as low a wage as 10s. 6d. weekly. The workers, indeed, suffer when trade is bad, but they do not gain in proportion when trade is good . . . . . .

Warehouse girls' wages, however, are no better than those of factory-workers. In a fairly decent house, a woman stitcher earns from 10s. and 11s. to 18s. a week on the piece-work system, and printers—girls who stencil on to the linen the perforated design—are paid as low as 7s. 6d. Ornamenters make about 12s. weekly.

The deadliest sin in the labour conditions of Ireland is neither the low wage paid to unskilled labourers nor that paid to women. It is the system under which boys and girls hardly out of their infancy are employed in the mills at a wage of 3s. 6d. a week. The child half-timer in Lancashire is often an object of sympathy. The plight of the Ulster half-timer, however, is infinitely more pitiable. In Lancashire the child really works half-time every day of the week and goes to school during the other part of the day. In Ulster the child works full time during three days in the week, and attends school on the remaining days. The results which follow, when children of twelve years old or thereabouts are kept working for ten hours a day during three days in the week in a humid atmosphere of from 70 to 80 degrees Fahrenheit, might have been foreseen. Vitality is slowly squeezed out of them, and it is hardly an exaggeration to say that from the age of 15 upwards they die like flies.

The death rate in Belfast among young people between the ages of 15 and 20 is double what it is in Manchester. That this is due neither to inherited lack of vitality not to the condition of Belfast houses is proved by the fact that in the first five years of their life children die less rapidly in Belfast than in Manchester. Miss Martindale,[*] who is as enviably free from the vice of dogmatism as she is from that of melodrama, believes that the over-crowded, ill-ventilated and insufficiently-warmed state of some of the schools may be a partial cause of the high deathrate among these boys and girls, but there can be little doubt that the half-time system is a ruling cause of such an unnatural rate of mortality.

Robert Lynd, *Home Life in Ireland* (London, 1904), pp 229-30.

a government inspector of factories.

Right: *Reeling linen yarn in a Belfast spinning mill (Lawrence Collection, National Library of Ireland)*

Below: *Ornamenting finished linen (Welch Collection, Ulster Museum)*

Robert Lynd was born in Belfast in 1879 and educated at the Royal Belfast Academical Institution and Queen's College (now Queen's University). He wrote a number of novels and travel books about Ireland. These include *The mantle of the emperor* (London, 1906) and *Rambles in Ireland* (London, 1912). A republican and Gaelic Leaguer from his youth, he also edited some of the works of James Connolly - *Labour in Ireland: Labour in Irish history, The reconquest of Ireland* (Dublin and London, 1917). However, his considerable renown as a writer rests not so much upon these works as on his essays, many of which were written during the time he was literary editor of the *News Chronicle*. He wrote under the pseudonym of Y.Y., and among his books of essays are *The art of letters* (London, 1920), and *Books and authors* (London, 1929). A number of his best essays were published in London in 1933 in the volume *Y.Y. An anthology of essays*, selected, with an introduction, by Eileen Squire. Robert Lynd died in 1949.

LINES ON PORTADOWN

Hail, Portadown! thou bonny gem,
    The rising star of Erin's Isle,
The seat of enterprising men,
    Who have caus'd thy trade to smile;

Who, by their increasing labour,
    Have made you a princely home,
Where the townsman and the stranger
    Are alike sweet friendship shown.

Through thee flow the lovely waters
    Of the far-famed river Bann,
Where thy social sons and daughters
    Spend convivial evenings on.

Proudly stand thy lofty buildings
    Once where nought but ruin stood,
Beautifi'd with costly gildings,
    Though yet in their infant bud.

Magic-like thy domes are rising,
    Tow'ring upwards to the sky;
And what makes the scene more prizing
    Is, no lordling's hand was nigh.

Thy factory-bells are heard each morn
    Chiming with the songster's lay,
Calling thousands to perform
    The various duties of the day.

Here the hand of trade is making
    Business marts triumphant rise;
While art with her a part has taken
    In the noble enterprise.

So let us unite together,
    And let discord die away;
Let us strive to help each other
    As we journey on life's way

Robert Donnolly, *Poetical works of Robert Donnolly*
(Portadown, 1882), pp 180-1.

Delft merchant, High Street, Portadown,
1892 (Sprott Collection, Portadown College)

A Portadown shopkeeper, 1892 (Sprott Collection, Portadown College)

Robert Donnolly was the author of hundreds of poems on people and places in Portadown and the surrounding area. These were often printed on broadsheets, sometimes illustrated by Donnolly himself. A native of Portadown, Co. Armagh, he was apparently a weaver by trade. He published two books of poetry; the first, *Poems on various subjects*, was published at Armagh in 1867 and the second in 1882 (see above). Some of his poems were written in praise of specific tradesmen and merchants. In his writing he speaks highly of the industrial growth taking place around him.

FOR a country where political agitations follow each other as rapidly as plagues in an Eastern City it is curious how little constructive thought we can show on the ideals of a rural civilization. But economic peace ought surely to have its victories to show as well as political war. I would a thousand times rather dwell on what men and women working together may do than on what may result from majorities at Westminster. The beauty of great civilization has been built up far more by people working together than by any corporate action of the State.

In these socialistic days we grow pessimistic about our own efforts and optimistic about the working of the legislature. I think we do right to expect great things from the State, but we ought to expect still greater things from ourselves. We ought to know full well that if the State did twice as much as it does we would never rise out of mediocrity among the nations unless we have unlimited faith in the power of our personal efforts, to raise and transform Ireland and unless we translate the faith into works.

The State can give a man an economic holding, but only the man himself can make it into an Earthly Paradise, and it is a dull business, un-worthy of a being made in the image of God, to grind away at work without some noble end to be served, some glowing ideal to be attained...............

"What dream shall we dream, or what labour shall we undertake?" you may ask, and it is right that those who exhort should be asked in what manner and how precisely they would have the listener act or think. I answer : the first thing to do is to create and realize the feeling for the community and break up the evil and petty isolation of man from man. This can be done by every kind of co-operative effort where combined action is better than individual action. The parish cannot take care of the child as well as the parents, but you will find in most of the labours of life combined action is more fruitful than individual action.

Some of you have found this out in many branches of agriculture, of which your dairying, agricultural, credit, poultry, and flax societies are witness. Some of you have combined to manufacture; some to buy in common; some to sell in common. Some of you have the common ownership of thousands of pounds' worth of expensive machinery. Some of you have carried the idea of co-operation for economic ends further, and have used the power which combination gives you to erect village halls and to have libraries of books, the windows through which the life and wonder and power of humanity can be seen. Some of you have light-heartedly, in the growing sympathy of unity, revived the dances and songs and sports which are the right relaxation of labour.

Some Irishwomen here and there have heard beyond the four walls in which so much of their lives are spent the music of a new day, and have started out to help and inspire the men and be good comrades to them; and, calling themselves United Irish**wo**men, they have joined, as the men have joined, to help their sisters who are in economic servitude, or who suffer from the ignorance and indifference to their special needs in life which pervade the administration of local government. We cannot build up a rural civilization in Ireland without the aid of Irish women. It will help life little if we have methods of the twentieth century in the fields and those of the fifth century in the home..........
Working so, we create the conditions in which the spirit of the community grows strong.

George Russell, *Co-operation and nationality* (Dublin, 1912), pp82-3, 88-91.

At first sight, this extract may seem a strange one to include for the poet George William Russell, or, as he was better known, AE. But in fact Russell had a considerable interest in economic affairs, especially in relation to the land. In 1897 he became an official of the Irish Agricultural Organization Society and from 1906 to 1923 he was editor of its magazine, *The Irish Homestead*. It is of course for his very considerable literary ability that Russell is best remembered. Born at Lurgan, Co. Armagh, in 1867, he moved at an early age to Dublin. He became one of the most influential members of the Irish literary revival at the turn of the century and wrote a large number of books of verse, stories and plays, nearly all of a mystical nature. Russell's play, *Deidre*, was staged in Dublin in 1902 by the Irish National Dramatic Company. His volume, *Collected poems*, was published in London in 1913 (2nd ed. London, 1926). Other writings include *The Candle of Vision* (London, 1918) and *Interpreters* (London, 1922). In addition to being a writer Russell was a painter, the subjects often being mystical ones like his poetry. He died in 1935.

Above: *The committee of the Irish Co-operative Women's Guild, York Street Branch, Belfast—part of Russell's co-operative movement but hardly rural (Mr. Fred Heatley's private collection)*

Above left: *This photograph of the creamery at Donemana, Co. Tyrone was taken around 1910. By this time the co-operative movement had become an important feature of the agricultural scene throughout Ireland. At the end of 1910 there were 881 local co-operative societies belonging to the Irish Agricultural Organization Society with a total membership of just under 95,000. (Cooper Collection, Public Record Office of Northern Ireland)*

OLD AND NEW

I see the older men
Of Ireland bent and bowed,
By marsh and rushy fen
Dig out from fibrous shroud
The peats, and shape the turf-stacks red
With centuries' slow rest beneath the bog,
Where rotted rivers hold in dead
Embrace both elk, and steed, and leafen log.
Up higher on the fold
Of living earth that lies
With healthy hill-fed mould
Thrown open to the skies,
I see the young men toil the full
Long day to tear the fragrant earth apart,
And fling the seed so beautiful
About their mother's unforgetting heart.

Shane Leslie, *Songs of Oriel* (Dublin, 1908), p. 37.

Turf cutting at Gortconny bog, Co. Antrim
(Welch Collection, Ulster Museum)

Sir John Randolph (Shane) Leslie, (1885-1971), from Glaslough, Co. Monaghan, was educated at Eton and Cambridge. He was a cousin of Sir Winston Churchill. He wrote a large number of biographies, histories, novels and poems. His volumes of poetry include *Verses in peace and war* (London, 1922), and *Poems and ballads* (London, 1933). He was keenly interested in ghosts and wrote several books about them - *Fifteen odd stories* (London, 1935), and *Shane Leslie's ghost book* (London, 1955), His other works include *The Oxford Movement* (London, 1933), and *George the Fourth* (London, 1926).

Out beyond the swaths the mowers toiled on, smitten pitilessly by the sun. Both were stripped to the shirt and trousers, neck-bands open, sleeves rolled high, hats pushed back upon nape and crown. Hughy's shirt was wet below the armpits, soaked about the neck and waist, clinging tight to his back as a cotton skin; but Peter's flapped dry as a bone. When Hughy, turning for a new swath, wiped his brow his arm glistened from wrist to elbow; but Peter's scraped over the parched wrinkles with a withered sound of dryness. The sun sucked at Peter unavailingly, warmed him as it might warm a stone, wrought nothing but freckles on the brown leanness of his arms; but Hughy it smote, working in him riot and ferment, boiling his blood, baking his bones, making him smoke along the stubble.

They worked hard, stopping only to whet scythes, or trudge to the drinking can, or turn down between the mounded rows, their feet crushing the eyes of fallen daisies, pressing the life from tumbled thistle and meadow-sweet, driving corncrakes in panic through the grass or crushing wounded frogs into the stubble.

The burden of work and of the day was heavy, but they bore it unmurmuringly; accepting it as they accepted most things—hunger and cold, pain and trouble, life and death—with an air of sullen indifference, of philosophic resignation to the inevitable—the inevitable before which your sapient ran cheerfully nor lingered to be kicked. They looked out upon the glories of earth and sky,. the wonders of sunshine and shade, with indifferent eyes, seeing only what a thousand times they had seen, and knew by heart, and hoped by God's mercy to see often again. It was just the trees with them, the crops, the grass, the hills and the cattle, the valleys and the meadows, the sun that shone and the men that worked.

S. F. Bullock, *Irish pastorals* (London, 1901), pp84-5.

Mowing corn at Toome, Co. Antrim (Green Collection, Ulster Folk Museum)

This extract comes from 'The mowers', a short story included in Shan F. Bullock's *Irish pastorals;* it is set in the Cavan-Fermanagh border countryside, as were many of his novels. Born in 1865 at Crom, Co. Fermanagh as John William Bullock, he was brought up around Crom Castle where his father was steward. He eventually went to London where he spent most of his life as a civil servant. For his work on the secretariat of the Irish Convention of 1917 he was awarded the M.B.E. His best known novels are *The loughsiders* (London, 1924), *Dan the dollar* (Dublin, 1907), and *The squireen* (London, 1903). He wrote an autobiographical volume entitled *After sixty years,* published in London in 1931. He also wrote poetry and a play, *Snow drop Jane,* which was produced in Belfast in 1915. He died in 1935.

Harvesters and a steam threshing machine around 1915 (Cooper Collection, Public Record Office of Northern Ireland)

These two girls at Glenshesk, Co. Antrim, are putting the finishing touches to 'lazy beds' of seed potatoes. The 'lazy beds' were made by digging ditches and putting the soil to one side on top of the seeds. This photograph probably dates from the late nineteenth century. (Welch Collection, Ulster Museum)

Joseph Campbell, or Seosamh MacCathmaoil as he was sometimes called, was born in Belfast in 1879. He was an early contributor to the Ulster Literary Theatre, his play, *The little cowherd of Slainge,* being performed by the Theatre in 1905. But it is undoubtedly for his poetry and songs that Campbell is best remembered. He drew much of his inspiration from the northern countryside, particularly the counties of Antrim and Donegal. Along with the musician Herbert Hughes he collected traditional Ulster songs; 'My Lagan love' is probably the best known of these. Many of his poems were religious in nature. In *The gilly of Christ* (Dublin, 1907), he set the life of Christ among the people and fields of Ulster's countryside. After spending some time in Dublin and London, Campbell settled in Co. Wicklow. His play, *Judgement,* was performed at the Abbey Theatre in 1911. Campbell was a staunch republican and was imprisoned during the Irish civil war. On being released in 1924 he went to the United States. In 1935 he returned to Co. Wicklow where he died in 1944. A collected edition of his poetry, *Poems of Joseph Campbell,* introduced by Austin Clarke, was published in Dublin in 1963.

HARVEST SONG

O reapers and gleaners,
Come dance in the sun:
The last sheaves are stooked
And the harvest is done.

The thistle-finch sings,
And the corn-plover cries,
And the bee and the moth
Flit about in the skies.

For Jesus has quickened
The seed in the mould,
And turned the green ears
Of the summer to gold.

The hill-folk all winter
Have clamoured for bread,
And here is enough
For a host to be fed!

Last year was a lean year,
And this is a fat,
And poor folk have cause
To be thankful for that.

So, reapers and gleaners,
Come dance in the sun,
And praise Mary's Child
That the harvest is done.

Joseph Campbell, *The rushlight*
(Dublin, 1906), p.54.

*This farmer in the Mourne mountains above Kilkeel,
Co. Down, is winnowing corn. Winnowing is the process of shaking or hand threshing corn to remove the
chaff from the head of corn. This scene was photographed around 1915. (Green Collection, Ulster Folk
Museum)*

Above: *A school classroom, location unknown. From the tidy
appearance of all the children it is clear they knew a photographer was coming to the school! (Public Record Office of
Northern Ireland)*

Right: *The master and pupils of Black's school, Strabane,
Co. Tyrone (Cooper Collection, Public Record Office of
Northern Ireland)*

THE school-house faced the Market Square. It was a dingy, dilapidated-looking building, both inside and out.

A few rude desks and forms, well worn, and diminishing in size, owing to well applied and constant whittling with jack-knives; the master's desk in the corner, together with the usual wall covering of maps and alphabetical charts, completed the furnishing of the apartment.

There was a distinct air of disorder and untidiness about the place—the same might be said regarding not a few of its inhabitants.

The master, David Grahame, commonly called "Fractions," owing to his recognised ability for land measuring, and the puzzling calculations connected therewith, was a tall, well-built, fresh-complexioned man, with a somewhat marked cast of features, keen grey eyes, prominent nose, and a firmly set mouth. His age may have been fifty-five.

Many were the stories told of his talents and versatility—all going to prove to what heights he might have risen, had good luck appointed him to a wider field.

Not only had he laid the groundwork of some eminent scholars, and accomplished not a few wonderful geometrical and algebraical feats, but he also possessed a smattering of legal knowledge, which enabled him to be of much service in the drawing up of wills and agreements. Added to all this "the Master" displayed a distinct aptitude for theological argument and debate, having had more than one wordy tussle with the minister himself: the minister, it is said, coming off a good second.

Archibald McIlroy, *When lint was in the field* (Belfast, 1897), pp15-16.

This description of a school and a teacher comes from reminiscences of his younger days by the author, Archibald McIlroy. Born at Ballyclare, Co. Antrim, he worked in the bank and in business. He was also a local councillor. He contributed to many magazines and was the author of several works and sketches describing Ulster life. His books include *The auld meeting house green* (Belfast, 1898), *A banker's love story* (London, 1901) and *The humour of Devil's Island* (Dublin, 1902). He was drowned in 1915 at the age of fifty-five on the *Lusitania*.

RUN DOWN

IN the grim dead end he lies, with passionless filmy
    eyes,
English Ned, with a hole in his head,
Staring up at the skies.

The engine driver swore as often he swore before —
    "I whistled him back from the flamin' track,
An' I could n't do no more."

The gaffer spoke through the 'phone "Platelayer
    Seventy-one
    Got killed to-day on the six-foot way,
By a goods on the city run.

    "English Ned was his name,
    No one knows whence he came,
    He didn't take mind of the road behind
    And none of us is to blame."

    They turned the slag in the bed
    To cover the clotted red,
    Washed the joints and the crimsoned points,
    And buried poor English Ned.

    In the drear dead end he lies,
    With the earth across his eyes,
    And a stone to say,
    How he passed away
    To a shift beyond the skies.

This photograph of railway workers was taken at Lifford in Co. Donegal around 1911 (Cooper Collection, Public Record Office of Northern Ireland)

Patrick MacGill, *Songs of the dead end* (London, 1913), p.132.

Born at Glenties, Co. Donegal, in 1891, Patrick MacGill left school at the age of 10. Four years later he emigrated to Scotland where he worked as a navvy, a platelayer and a labourer. His first volume of poems about the life of a navvy, *Gleanings from a navvy's scrapbook* (Greenock, 1911), was immediately popular and was followed by *Songs of a navvy* (Windsor, 1912), and *Songs of the dead end* (London, 1913). In the next year he wrote *Children of the dead end*, published in London, a semi-autobiographical novel set in the farmlands of the Lagan countryside (north-east Donegal) and in Scotland. During the 1914-18 war, he served in the London Irish Rifles, an experience which prompted him to write a number of books depicting the horror of war - *The great push - an episode of the Great War* (London, 1916), *Soldier songs* (London, 1917) and *The amateur army* (London, 1915). His play about war, *Suspense,* was published in London in 1930. Other works of importance include *Maureen* (London, 1921), *The glen of Carra* (London, 1934) and *The rat pit* (London, 1915). MacGill went to the United States in 1930. He died in 1963.

An office of the Belfast Ropework Company on the Newtownards Road, Belfast, January 1899 (Linenhall Library)

BY THE WATER

The last of the coal schooners about 1893 at the Queen's Quay, Belfast. (Welch Collection, Ulster Museum)

SEA WRACK

THE wrack was dark an' shiny where it floated in
    the sea,
There was no one in the brown boat but only him
    an' me;
Him to cut the sea wrack, me to mind the boat,
An' not a word between us the hours we were afloat.
      The wet wrack,
      The sea wrack,
      The wrack was strong to cut.

We laid it on the grey rocks to wither in the sun,
An' what should call my lad then, to sail from
    Cushendun?
With a low moon, a full tide, a swell upon the deep,
Him to sail the old boat, me to fall asleep.
    The dry wrack,
    The sea wrack,
    The wrack was dead so soon.

There' a fire low upon the rocks to burn the wrack
    to kelp
There' a boat gone down upon the Moyle, an' sorra
    one to help!
Him beneath the salt sea, me upon the shore,
By sunlight or moonlight we'll lift the wrack no
    more
      The dark wrack,
      The sea wrack,
      The wrack may drift ashore.

Moira O'Neill, *Songs of the Glens of Antrim* (London, 1900), pp10-11.

Moira O'Neill was the pen-name of Nesta Higginson, later Mrs. Nesta Skrine. Born at Cushendun in the Glens of Antrim, she is best known for her songs and poems of the Glens. The first edition of *Songs of the Glens of Antrim* was published in London in 1900, and ran into many editions and impressions. In 1921, also in London, *More songs of the Glens of Antrim* was brought out. Earlier writings include *An Easter vacation* (London, 1893), and *The elf errant* (London, 1895). A collected volume of her poems was published in 1933 - *Collected poems of Moira O'Neill* (London). She eventually went to Canada but returned to Ireland to live in Co. Wicklow, where she died in 1955 at the age of 90.

Left: *Seaweed gatherers at work near Fair Head, Co. Antrim. Notice the jetty for the Ballycastle coal field. (Welch Collection, Ulster Museum)*

Below: *Burning seaweed for kelp in an Antrim coast glen. Materials extracted from the kelp, as the burnt seaweed was know, were used in the production of bleaching materials and glass. (Green Collection, Ulster Folk Museum)*

NANCY [Energetically]: I'll have the kettle on the boil in two twos. [During the foregoing the minister has gone over to Bell, and shakes her hand, which he holds long and tenderly, looking steadily into her face. Bell is downcast.]

MINISTER [With a half-guilty start moving over to side of table]: No, thank you, I'll not mind.

JOHNNY [Interrogatively, glancing at clock]: You must be cold, out at such a late hour in this weather. [He looks searchingly across at Bell.]

NANCY [Taking down tea-caddy]: Aye, a good cup o' tay will warm you up.

MINISTER: Thank you all the same, but I'll not stay now. [Nancy puts the caddy back with an air of disappointment.] I came round by the quay and heard some of the men talking of going off and trying a night at the fishing.

NANCY: The weather's not settled yet; maybe it's only a calm between storms.

MINISTER: One of them urged that they should take the big sail they used when the "Annie" won the race last autumn at the regatta.

JOHNNY [Angrily to Nancy] It'll be that young scape-grace Rob [Bell starts] He's up to every divilment [To minister], sav'n your presence.

He nearly swamped himself in the yawl the other day tryin' how much wind she would stand without sinkin' the lee gunnel.

MINISTER: I couldn't make them out in the darkness, as the beached boats were between them and me, but I heard the same voice say, as if to itself: "It's win or lose tonight."
[Bell agitated, but pleased.]

JOHNNY: The racin's never out of his head.

NANCY [Coming from fire after taking kettle off and hanging bellows]: It's dangerous work at this time o' year.

MINISTER [Moving towards Nancy]: So I thought I'd just look in and give you a word of warning. [Bell is listening at the door, and her face lights up as she appears to recognise a footstep. Minister shakes hands with Nancy.]

NANCY: We're obleged to you. Johnny'll put sense into Rob or any o' the boat's crew that comes to take him from his fireside, and his wife and chile at such a time and in such weather.

J. H. Cousins, *The racing lug* from Robert Hogan and James Kilroy (ed.), *Lost plays of the Irish renaissance* (Dixon, California, 1970), pp 42-3.

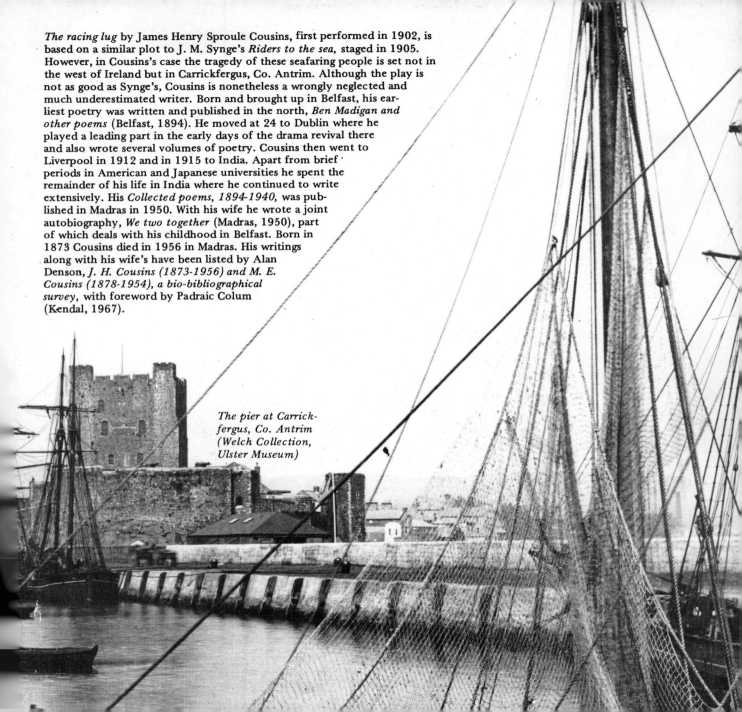

The racing lug by James Henry Sproule Cousins, first performed in 1902, is based on a similar plot to J. M. Synge's *Riders to the sea*, staged in 1905. However, in Cousins's case the tragedy of these seafaring people is set not in the west of Ireland but in Carrickfergus, Co. Antrim. Although the play is not as good as Synge's, Cousins is nonetheless a wrongly neglected and much underestimated writer. Born and brought up in Belfast, his earliest poetry was written and published in the north, *Ben Madigan and other poems* (Belfast, 1894). He moved at 24 to Dublin where he played a leading part in the early days of the drama revival there and also wrote several volumes of poetry. Cousins then went to Liverpool in 1912 and in 1915 to India. Apart from brief periods in American and Japanese universities he spent the remainder of his life in India where he continued to write extensively. His *Collected poems, 1894-1940*, was published in Madras in 1950. With his wife he wrote a joint autobiography, *We two together* (Madras, 1950), part of which deals with his childhood in Belfast. Born in 1873 Cousins died in 1956 in Madras. His writings along with his wife's have been listed by Alan Denson, *J. H. Cousins (1873-1956) and M. E. Cousins (1878-1954), a bio-bibliographical survey*, with foreword by Padraic Colum (Kendal, 1967).

The pier at Carrickfergus, Co. Antrim (Welch Collection, Ulster Museum)

Ardglass fishing boats returning to harbour (Lawrence Collection, National Library of Ireland)

Samuel Kennedy Cowan was one of six northern poets who had a selection of their works published together in 1896. Born at Lisburn, Co. Antrim, in 1850, Cowan graduated from Dublin University. He was probably most renowned in his day as a writer of Christmas-card verse. Legend has it that he regularly wrote up to 400 rhymes and verses for a single Christmas. Many of his lyrics were set to music by composers including Sir Arthur Sullivan. Among his volumes of poetry are *Poems* (London, 1873), *Victoria the good* (Newry, 1897), and *From Ulster's hills* (Belfast, 1913). Besides all this Cowan was a major in the militia. He died in 1918.

Three fishwives from Newcastle, Co. Down (Green Collection, Ulster Folk Museum)

DUNDRUM BAR

THEY sailed away with never a care,
　Under the light of moon and star,
For the tide was full and the wind was fair
　At Dundrum Bar.
Five good fishermen, steady and brave,
Ready to battle with wind and wave,
　Each for his own,
With their nets aboard, all trim and strong,
They sailed away with cheer and song,
Sou'-sou'-east, toward Annalong,
　Where deep seas moan.

Lamps on the land through the live-long night,
　Steadily gleaming, broad and far,
Streamed, like a golden lane of light,
　Thro' Dundrum Bar.
Beacon-lamps of home were they,
Trimmed by true hands lovingly,
　Each for her own;
Lamps, alas! that, thro' the dark,
Never again shall light their bark,
Lying alone and low and stark,
　Where deep seas moan!

All night long and the livelong day,
　Watching, waiting, each for her own,
Gazed they fondly, and far away,
　Where deep seas moan.
Gazed till, lo! before the gale,
Was it sail, or seaweed pale,
　Or shattered spar
Saw they, drifting, still and white,
All in the golden lane of light
Shed by the shore-lamps, shining bright,
Thro' Dundrum Bar?

It was neither seaweed pale,
　Neither sail nor shattered spar,
Drifting ashore before the gale,
　Thro' Dundrum Bar.
Nay; but the corse of one was it
Whose ghost the lamps of love had lit
　Back to his own;
For love from love no death can keep,
For love is mighty, and love is deep
And vast as the graves of them that sleep
　Where deep seas moan.

S. K. Cowan, *Sung by six. Collected poems of six poets* (Belfast, 1896), pp 51-3.

Regatta day at Bangor, Co. Down (Lawrence Collection, National Library of Ireland)

NORTH SEA BUBBLES

In the South there dwelt an Earl
Who possessed a fine 'Black Pearl'
Of goodly lines and build was she,
Her size in tons 'three forty three'.

The Earl had once expressed desire
His jewel rare to let on hire,
So, to a Celt on pleasure bent,
His well beloved pearl he lent.

Then Captain Bond so staunch and true
His mates, his boatswain and the crew-
Twenty-five hands on board, all hearty-
Were joined from Redburn by our party.

The Irishman, his wife and son,
John Harrison and Arthur Dunn,
Miss Fowler, too, of Rahinstown,
In hunting field of great renown.

From Aberdeen the good ship sails,
Not fearing North Sea storm or gales,
And soon we reach the shore beyond
Secure, and safely 'under Bond'.

(cont.)

R. G. Dunville, *North Sea bubbles* (Belfast, not dated), pp13-15.

Members of the Annesley family from Castlewellan, Co. Down, aboard their yacht on the way to Cowes, 1893 (Annesley Collection, Public Record Office of Northern Ireland)

Robert Grimshaw Dunville (1838-1910) was a member of the famous Dunville whiskey family whose advertisements in Ulster newspapers at the end of the nineteenth century assured readers that their stocks of whiskey in Belfast were the largest in the world! Besides being a whiskey distiller, he was an aspiring poet. These aspirations, however, received little acknowledgment. In his *Dictionary of Irish poets*, D. J. O'Donoghue mentions a volume of poetry called *The voyage*, published by him in 1891, which, O'Donoghue remarks, he 'sensibly suppressed' after its publication. Smarting, no doubt, from the criticism of this first book, Dunville had his second book, *North Sea bubbles*, published privately for friends. As can be seen from the above passage, it was hardly a serious work. But had he produced this book for children, there can have been little doubt of its success. *North Sea bubbles* deals with a trip he made with his family and some friends from their home at Redburn, near Holywood, Co. Down, in a boat called the *Black Pearl*. The book is pleasantly illustrated by the author and would have fascinated young readers.

CASSIE: May I bring in the bicycle out o' the rain? Dear sakes, what's the matter, Ellen! Have ye bad news?

ELLEN: Ach, no! But she's getting old, and it doesn't take much to vex her. She's fretting, like, because I'm going to America, and she'd like me to stay here. But it's no use thinking o't.

CASSIE (*Propping bicycle against dresser and coming up to Mary*):- Ach, now, Mrs. Macauley, don't you be taking on like that; don't now. What's going to America that it should fret ye? What else does anybody be doing in the glens? Isn't it three out of four, and five out of six, and six out of seven in every house that goes? There's nothing else for them to do. This is a poor country, and out there there's plenty o' work and lashings o' money, and why wouldn't they go! I'm real thankful I'm out there myself, so I am, and it's thankful ye should be that Ellen's going for she'll do fine.

MARY: I'm not thankful, then; I'm sore displeased at her, Cassie, leaving me me lone and going off to sport herself in America, or the dear knows where. It's not you that knows what it is to have your childer glad to leave ye, and ye may be thankful this day that ye're not married. Ye'll never have the heart-break that I have, and it's well for ye.

CASSIE: 'Deed that's just what I'm thinking meself, when I'm back here and see the empty houses and the old men and women that's filling the country. I wouldn't live here not for all the gold in America. But come now, Mrs. Macauley, rise off that trunk and come and sit by the fire. You'll be better so. (*She leads Mrs. Macauley to chair by fire and sits down beside her*). Listen now, and I'll tell ye. Ellen's got the wish to go to America, and don't you be stopping her. What would she do here at all at all! Shure this is no country for them as is young and stirring. She'll send you back more money in a year than ever she'd make in all her life in Ireland. Don't ye know that?

MARY: It's me daughter's company, not the money I'd want. Why wouldn't she stay here and marry a decent man, and wouldn't that be better nor pounds and pounds? Ye know it would.

M. E. Dobbs, *She's going to America*, included in *Village plays* (Dundalk, 1920), pp37-8.

Right: *Belfast Quays around 1910. Notice both the sail and steam boats. (Lawrence Collection, National Library of Ireland)*

Below: *American liner at Moville, Co. Donegal, probably around 1890. This boat stopped to take on passengers from Derry brought by tender from Moville. (Lawrence Collection, National Linrary of Ireland) In 1883 over 15,000 people left through Derry for Canada and the U.S.A.*

This play, *She's going to America*, set in the Glens of Antrim, was first performed at Cushendall in September 1912. It deals with the problem of emigration and its effects on the local community. In the introduction to the volume containing this and three other plays, the authoress, Margaret Emmeline Dobbs, explains that they were written specially for a company of village actors and were designed to meet the difficulties of production in a country district. Three of the plays were staged at Cushendall in a hay loft turned into a long narrow hall, with stage, scenery and lighting of local construction. Margaret Dobbs was born in Co. Antrim and spent much of her life in the Glens of Antrim. She was an Irish scholar of some note. She died in 1961 aged 88.

QUAYS. BELFAST. 4745. W.L.

Members of the Belfast Naturalist Field Club on a boat trip on Lough Erne, Co. Fermanagh, July 1892. The B.N.F.C. was founded in 1863. Along with the Belfast Natural History and Philosophical Society, founded in 1821, it has done much to promote the study of the geology, botany, archaeology and history of the province. (R. W. Welch, Praeger Album, Royal Irish Academy)

A SONG OF FREEDOM

In Cavan of little lakes,
As I was walking with the wind,
And no one seen beside me there,
There came a song into my mind :
It came as if the whispered voice
Of one, but none of humankind,
Who walked with me in Cavan then,
And he invisible as wind.

On Urris, of Inish-Owen,
As I went up the mountainside,
The brook that came leaping down
Cried to me, for joy it cried;
And when from off the summit far
I looked o'er land and water wide,
I was more joyous than the brook
That met me on the mountainside.

To Ara, of Connacht's isles,
As I went sailing o'er the sea,
The wind's word, the brook's word,
The wave's word, was plain to me—
"As we are, though she is not.
As we are shall Banba be—
There is no King can rule the wind
There is no fetter for the sea."

ALICE MILLIGAN

Henry Morgan (ed.), *Poems by Alice Milligan* (Dublin, 1954), P. 1.

Born at Omagh, Co. Tyrone, about 1866, Alice Milligan was educated in Belfast and London. She founded and edited with Ethna Carbery, the Belfast published magazine, the *Shan Van Vocht,* which, for the three years that it ran, had an important influence on Irish republicanism. She also wrote several novels and plays as well as books of poetry. The poem given here was first published in 1904. She died in 1953.

Mermen discovered in Lough Oughter, Co. Cavan, by the B.N.F.C. What eventually happened to these mermen is unfortunately not revealed in the Club's records! (Welch Collection, Ulster Museum)

Castle Place, Belfast, about 1908 (Lawrence Collection, National Library of Ireland)

Belfast shipyards 1910. S.S. Olympic and S.S. Titanic are both nearly completed. (Hogg Collection, Ulster Museum)

Donegall Place, Belfast, around 1908. The new City Hall was opened in 1906. (Lawrence Collection, National Library of Ireland)

Belfast—when you reach it—is not calculated to charm the eye. It has the features of any English manufacturing town so far as its buildings are concerned, and the finest structures it can show (without disparaging its handsome Town Hall) are the vast fabrics which rise in the dockyards, such ships as have never been built in the world before—marvels of symmetry and strength. To see them in the building up is to watch, perhaps, the most impressive exhibition of human skill and energy.

Stephen Gwynn, *Ulster* (London, 1911), p.15.

Stephen Lucius Gwynn (1864-1950) was born in Dublin but spent many of his early and most formative years in Co. Donegal. From 1906 until 1918 he was a Nationalist M.P. He was the author of a large number of novels, Irish travel books, biographies and volumes of poetry. In 1899 he wrote a popular Ulster travelogue, *Highways and byways in Donegal and Antrim* (London). His *Collected poems* were published in 1923 in London. Among Gwynn's novels and short story collections are *John Maxwell's marriage* (London, 1903), and *The glade in the forest*. (Dublin, 1907). He also wrote an interesting autobiography called *Experiences of a literary man* (London, 1926).

These photographs are from an album about a Belfast temperance missionary around 1910. Above is a young man who has learnt the better of his ways and is signing the pledge under the watchful eyes of the missionary and a policeman! Top right is the missionary (on the right) in a public house on the Shankill Road and below right is a court scene. (D. H. Hogg, Linenhall Library)

Bernard Magennis (1833-1911) was born at Ballybay, Co. Monaghan. He was a national school teacher for a time, and wrote verse in newspapers such as the *Dundalk Democrat* and the *Northern Whig*. He lived for a number of years in New York and Lancashire. A prominent temperance advocate, he edited a Dublin paper, *The Social Mirror and Temperance Advocate*. His books include *Anti humbug, or Mansion House banquets midst Ireland's poverty* , (Manchester, 1890) and *The catapult, a satire* (Dublin, 1897). Other members of the Magennis family, especially Peter Magennis,, were well-known poets in south-west Ulster.

THE BOYS OF OUR DAY

We live in an age of great progress 'tis clear,
Though some think our progress doth crab-like appear,
And assert that each step in advance that we take
Another still backward we slip—by *mistake;*
And so be where we started it's plain to my mind,
Neither moving an inch, nor yet stopping behind;
Having prefaced thus far, I'll proceed to portray,
As I find them before me, the boys of our day.

See that urchin who out from his pocket doth draw
An old dhudeen pipe which he sticks in his jaw!
He wants with *men's* age, not his own to keep pace,
As you'll see by his wizen'd and smoke begrimed face.
Mark his impudent phiz and his comical leers,
Though he's little yet over a half score of years!
He's so fast from his nature he's run clean away,
This specimen bright of the boys of our day!

. . . .

There are others who sit in a corner obscure,
And call for their glasses of Jameson's pure;
With a smack on their lips and delight in each soul,
They drain to the dregs the accursed damning bowl,
'Till the roses of youth on their cheek soon have fled,
And the spring-time of life scarcely blooms 'till 'tis dead,
While all that is pure is corroding away,
And in crime they grow hoary, these boys of our day.

They prefer such amusements as *manly* are thought,
But the pleasures *they* bring oft too dearly are bought;
Those pleasures are false, vicious pastimes impart,
And leave still behind them a sting in the heart;
Behold the poor waifs and the strays that now roam
The streets of the cities abroad and at home.
What brought them to that? If they speak truth, they'll say
Parental neglect of the boys of our day!

Bernard Magennis, *Lamh Dearg or the Red Hand*
(Dublin, 1887), pp 147-9.

Uladh means Ulster. It is still often necessary to state as much : we intend to insist. Draw an imaginary line across Ireland from that great bight, Donegal Bay, in the west, to Carlingford Lough, on the east, and draw it not too rigidly : north of that you have Ulster. This Ulster has its own way of things, which may be taken as the great contrast to the Munster way of things, still keeping on Irish lands.

Cities like Londonderry and Belfast have drawn all its best energies towards them. And though of late years the city has been more a stumbling block to the right intellectual and artistic progress of the country yet, in spite of influences and disabilities operating against it, a certain characteristic temperamental and mental trend has been lent to the town by the country, and a certain local intellectual activity has persisted there. We wish to locate this, and to afford it an outlet in literary expression.

Exactly what that local temperament and artistic aptitude are *Uladh* wants to discuss. *Uladh* would also influence them, direct and inform them. And as the Theatre is the most essential of all art activities, and the surest test of a people's emotional and intellectual vitality, *Uladh* starts out as the organ of the Theatre, the Ulster Literary Theatre, but proposes to be as irrelevant to that movement and its topics as is deemed necessary.

We recognise at the outset that our art of the drama will be different from that other Irish art of drama which speaks from the stage of the Irish National Theatre in Dublin, where two men, W. B. Yeats and Douglas Hyde, have set a model in Anglo-Irish and Gaelic plays with a success that is surprising and exhilarating. Dreamer, mystic, symbolist, Gaelic poet and propagandist have all spoken on the Dublin stage, and a fairly defined local school has been inaugurated. We in Belfast and Ulster also wish to set up a school; but there will be a difference.

At present we can only say that our talent is more satiric than poetic. That will probably remain the broad difference between the Ulster and the Leinster schools. But when our genius arrives, as he must

sooner or later, there is no accounting for what extraordinary tendency he may display. Our business is, however, to plod along gathering matter for his use, practising methods, perfecting technique, and training actors.

We have most to fear for the young men in that, if they do not find an outlet in Ulster, they will either go away, or gravitate upon the sloblands of American or English magazine work, which is purely commercial and has no pretention to literature whatever. It expresses nothing, means nothing; it aims at being sixpence-worth. We do not aim at being sixpence-worth; we aim at being priceless, for honesty and and good purpose are priceless. If we do not attain to all this, we shall at least attain to something unique in Ulster, smacking of the soil, the winds on the uplands, the north coast, the sun and the rain, and the long winter evenings.

Uladh will be non-sectarian and non-political; each article will be signed by the writer as an expression of his own individual views; other views may be put forward in another number. In any case, our pages will be kept free from the party-cries of mob and clique and market-place. Honesty in all matters of taste and opinion will, we hope, characterise our matter. Our contributors are mostly young men, of all sects and all grades of political opinion.

The journal will be run on broad propagandist lines. Propagandism on broad lines, we think, is desirable at this juncture. There is a strong undercurrent of culture in the North, and this we will endeavour to tap, and, if possible, turn into native channels. As a good Ulsterman, and a friend of this venture, has truly said: "We have it to effect a great deal—the voice of the Press is far-reaching. We may roll the stone that has been only pushed at by others. Then will the heroes of the North ride forth again: at present they only sleep within the cavern of dark prejudice and ignorance and distrust."

If we succeed in accomplishing this much, if we roll the stone, if it is in our power to awaken the heroes to activity and the people to sympathy and life, surely our existence will be justified.

Above left: *Forrest Reid - novelist (Mr. Stephen Gilbert's private collection)*

Above right: *Francis Joseph Bigger - antiquarian (R.W. Welch. Praeger Album, Royal Irish Academy)*

Below: *Scene from an Ulster Literary Theatre production of Rutherford Mayne's The turn of the road. The actors from left to right are John Campbell, Lily Hughes, J. Storey, Lewis Purcell and W. R. Gordon. (Mr. S. H. Bell's private collection)*

Uladh i, no. 1 (Nov. 1904), pp 1-3.

The extract on the right is from the opening editorial of the Belfast Literary magazine, *Uladh*. Although it ran for only 4 numbers its contributors included notable writers such as Robert Lynd, Forrest Reid, Carl Hardebeck, Bulmer Hobson, Francis Joseph Bigger, AE, Alice Milligan and George and Norman Morrow. One of its purposes was to promote the Ulster Literary Theatre which was founded in 1904 and ran until 1934. Various factors contributed to the Theatre's failure to equal the Abbey Theatre in Dublin. Prominent no doubt amongst these factors were lack of really outstanding writers like Yeats and Synge, failure to find permanent premises, absence of wealthy patrons, inadequate publishing and bookselling facilities, and a certain puritanical attitude in the north towards the theatre. Nonetheless the Ulster Literary Theatre did have considerable success and was responsible for bringing to the fore important playwrights like Rutherford Mayne.

Above: *Bishop Street, Derry, in the 1880s. At the end of the street can be seen the old Corporation Hall. (Robert French, Linenhall Library)*

Below: *Waterloo Place. Derry, around 1905 (Lawrence Collection, National Library of Ireland)*

Although born in Co. Wicklow in 1818, Mrs. Cecil Frances Alexander was closely associated with Derry city; she lived in Bishop Street from 1867 to 1895 when her husband was Bishop of Derry and Raphoe. She was a prolific and very able writer of hymns, many of which are still popular today, such as 'There is a green hill far away' and 'Once in royal David's City'; the first of these is supposed to have been written as she sat in her study looking out over the Derry hills. At this time there were a number of prominent hymn writers in Ulster. In 1896, the year after her death, a collected volume of Mrs. Alexander's poetry and hymns was published in London. Both her husband, William Alexander, and their daughter, Eleanor, were also well known writers.

ST. PATRICK'S BREASTPLATE

I BIND unto myself to-day
    The strong Name of the Trinity,
By invocation of the same,
    The Three in One and One in Three.

I bind this day to me for ever,
    By pow'r of faith, Christ's Incarnation;
His baptism in Jordan river;
    His death on Cross for my salvation;
His bursting from the spicèd tomb;
    His riding up the heav'nly way;
His coming at the day of doom;
    I bind unto myself to-day.

I bind unto myself to-day
    The virtues of the star-lit heaven,
The glorious sun's life-giving ray,
    The whiteness of the moon at even,
The flashing of the lightning free,
    The whirling wind's tempestuous shocks,
The stable earth, the deep salt sea,
    Around the old eternal rocks.

. . . .

Christ be with me, Christ within me,
    Christ behind me, Christ before me,
Christ beside me, Christ to win me,
    Christ to comfort and restore me,
Christ beneath me, Christ above me,
    Christ in quiet, Christ in danger,
Christ in hearts of all that love me,
    Christ in mouth of friend and stranger.

I bind unto myself the Name,
    The strong Name of the Trinity;
By invocation of the same,
    The Three in One, and One in Three.
Of Whom all nature hath creation:
    Eternal Father, Spirit, Word:
Praise to the Lord of my salvation,
    Salvation is of Christ the Lord.

Versified from the Irish by C. F. Alexander, *Poems* (London, 1896), pp 59-62.

THE ROYAL VISIT TO IRELAND
Letter from " Robin" to H.R.H. Prince Albert Victor
(Afterwards Duke of Clarence).

Ballycuddy, County Down,
May the tenth, 18 and 89.

"Dear Prince Albert Victor,

A'm prood tae heer that ye ir railly cumin' tae see Bilfast agen. Mony an' mony a time Peggy an' me haes been crackin' aboot ye since the last time that ye cummed wi' yer da an' ma. There wuz yin thing aboot ye, dear Prince, that struck Peggy mair nor ocht else, an' that was this : Ye'll hae min' o' that terble wat day that cummed on; weel, whun the fowk wuz cheerin' ower ocht ye sut in the kerridge wi' yer hat aff, an' the rain teemin' on ye like oot o' dishes. Peggy said ye wur a guid waen, an' wud make a gran' King sum day, jist if ye wudnae forget yersel' and grow prood. "Peggy, dear " sez I, "rale nobility is niver prood; it's only empty, ignerant upstarts that forgets themsels."

Hooaniver, pittin' that tae yin side, A'm prood, as A said afore, that yer cummin' back tae Bilfast. It shews that ye likit it whun ye wur there afore,' and' it shews at the same time that yer a wise, studdy young man whun yer royal Da an' Ma ir no afeerd tae trust ye awa' oot o' their sicht sae far.

A hope, dear Prince, ye'll no' feel affendit wi' me acause A tak' the liberty o' writin' ye this letter. A hae kent a' yer femily weel since A wuz a boy at Skule, an' A hae iver taen a great interest in the conserns o' the Royal Femily. A'm gaun up tae see ye, ov coorse, an' what fur noo? In echteen hunner an' foarty nine, whun yer Granda an' Granma cummed till Bilfast, A wuz there tae cheer wi' the tither fowk. Yer dear Granma didne ken me then, but she's a grate freen o' mine noo. They tell me ye redd the story A writ aboot me bein' interduced till the Queen in Glescoe last yeer; an' then ye ken that yer Da an' me ir auld akwantenances an' brither Freemasons. Shew him this letter, an' he'll tell ye a' aboot me an' whaur A leev.

. . . .

There'll harly be a chance o' my gettin' a aurd wi' ye while yer ower, there'll be sich a wheen o' the gran' fowk roon ye iverywhaur ye gang. Weel, weel, A maun pit up wi' the dissappoint, but ig A had ten minnits wi' ye

Part of the crowd at the city hall for the unveiling of Queen Victoria's statue in 1903 by King Edward VII (Welch Collection, Ulster Museum)

A wud gie ye a wheen hints that micht be usefu' till ye.

Dear Prince, A'm feered ye'll be tired readin' by this time, so A maun stap. The dear man, if ye wud cum doon to Bangor fur a day but the fowk wud like it. Ye cud hae a birl on the Switchback Railway, an' then ye cud see the Masonic Hall, an' the waterworks, an' a wheen ither places.

Wi' sincere and kind respekts frae me an' mine tae you an' yours,

A remain, Yer humble, loyal, an' law-abidin' servant,

Rabin Gordon."

W. G. Lyttle, *Robin's readings; part 1 - 3* (Belfast), pp 53-5.

Born at Newtownards, Co. Down, in 1844, Wesley Guard Lyttle was known as 'Robin', the author of a large number of poems and sketches in the dialect of a Co. Down farmer. In this character he used to give public readings which were extremely popular. In published form, *Robin's readings* ran through many editions. He also wrote several novels using a Co. Down dialect - *Sons of the sod* (Bangor, 1886) and *Betsy Gray, a tale of ninety-eight,* which was republished recently (Newcastle, Co. Down, 1968). As well as writing, Lyttle had a varied career which included running a Bangor newspaper, the *North Down and Bangor Gazette,* and he was one of the first to teach shorthand in Belfast. He died in 1896.

Some of the decorations in Donegall Square for the royal visit to Belfast in 1885. The White Linenhall has been specially decorated. Note the interesting writings on the arch. (R. W. Welch, Linenhall Library)

NEW TRAMWAYS COMMITTEE

AN IMAGINARY MEETING

WHO'LL BE CHAIRMAN?

The newly appointed members of the Tramways Committee met at the Town Hall the other day to appoint their chairman and make preliminary arrangements, when there was a full attendance. The proceedings were animated, if not interesting, and are fully reported below.

SIR SAMUEL BLACK—"Your first business is to appoint a chairman, and following my usual custom, I would suggest that you elect my old friend, Sir Dan——" (Loud cries of "No dictation," "You've played that game too long," &c., &c.

(Collapse of Sir Samuel temporarily.)

Alderman John M'Cormick is, as chairman of the Law Committee, moved to the chair in order to conduct the election.

Alderman JOHN M'CORMICK— "My Lord Mayor, Sir Daniel, and both Sir Roberts, and also gentlemen, this is the proudest moment of my life. Still, I shall not unnecessarily detain you by any simple words of mine, and will therefore be brief—ed. (hear, hear!) Before asking for nominations for the chairmanship, you will permit me to say in the very fewest of polysyllabic dithyrambics that such an unparalleled concatenation of the most brilliant intellectual attainments as are personified in the prominent personages composing the corruscation to be known henceforward as the Municipal Tramways Committee could not be equalled outside that noble city whose proud motto is *'Pro tanto quid retribuamus'.*"

Councillor M'INNES. — "Rats."

Ald. JOHN M'CORMICK—"I beg your pardon. Permit me to finish. To proceed then, we are not limited in our field of choice. The transincorporation of the street tramways system will effect a perfect metampsychosis in our conditions of vehicular traffic which no inconceivable predetermination can relieve from uncertainty. It is, therefore, your duty to select a member whose character shall be ascendant, predominant, commanding, controlling, regnant, sovereign, superior, and supreme to all such paltry considerations as laying lines economically, or such twopenny halfpenny trivialities as *halfpenny fares.* I know of no one, I say I know of no one in your number who fulfils all those conditions. Yet perhaps I exaggerate. There is ONE, but modesty and my position forbids me mentioning him."

Councillor W. MACARTNEY.—What about the deputations?

At this stage enter Councillors J. N. M'Cammond, James M'Entee, and Alderman W. Harper, the former singing—
"We'd a high old spree,
Me and M'Entee,
and the Alderman—
"We had, by gum-um-um."

Alderman Sir JAMES HENDERSON —"I quite concur in every word which Alderman John M'Cormick has excellently mentioned in his most excellent speech. Indeed, I think he put the matter in a most excellent way, but I do not see why his modesty or position should have prevented him mentioning my name, since it was evidently me whom he referred to."

Councillor WM. MACARTNEY — "What about the deputations?"

Alderman HARPER—"I'm sorry I came in a little late, but surely the Committee will not pass over one for the chairmanship who has the very highest qualifications." (Chorus of "Who? Who?") The Alderman, continuing — "Names, my Lord Mayor, names are unnecessary. I refer to the senior Alderman, the senior member of the Corporation present—one who, in the words of the poet, has
'With contemplative view surveyed mankind and womankind from China to Peru,'
and—may I say—picked up and dropped again a good few half-guineas during the process."

Councillor WM. MACARTNEY — "What about the deputations?"

Sir DANIEL—"Oh! d—— the deputations!"

Alderman WM. M'CORMICK (Falls) —"Are we never going to get down to business? We cannot all be chairman, so I wonder how it would do to co-opt an outsider. What price the Bishop? He has a great name for managing things,"

Sir JEAMES—"All betting news is strictly prohibited except in the most excellent columns of my most excellent newspaper."

Major Councillor CUNNINGHAM— "Aw! it-er is a gweat pity my Awldehman —I wefer to Awldehman Wobinson—is not heah. He has a vewy high opinion of me, and in my mititawy capacity-er I am accustomed to command-er."

Councillor W. MACARTNEY — "What about the depu——"

He is immediately and ignominiously removed by "James," Sergeant-at-Mace.

Councillor M'INNES—"Now, if you-'re nearly all done praising yourselves, I would like to make a nomination which I am sure will meet with unanimous approval. (Question.) Our chairman, whoever he may be, must be the embodiment of tact —(hear, hear!)—moderation—(hear, hear!) — suavity, courtesy, and consideration for the feelings of others. (Applause). I therefore have much pleasure in moving that Councillor William Walker——"

(Exeunt M'Innes gallantly defending himself against a storm of ink-pots; and break-up of the meeting in confusion.)

(It is long odds that they will be compelled to adopt old Sir Samuel's suggestion ultimately.)

Nomad's Weekly, no. 256, 18 June 1904.

Tram at the Whitehouse terminus, Dec. 1905 (A. R. Hogg, Linenhall Library). Horse drawn trams were introduced to Belfast in 1872 and replaced by electric trams in 1905.

Nomad's Weekly was a weekly Belfast satirical magazine first brought out in 1899 and which ran until 1914. During this time,, under the editorship of Alfred S. Moore it mercilessly satirized politicians, churchmen, trade union officials, corporation councillors and businessmen. No person or institution was safe from its searching columns. It led the field in many areas of social reform such as shorter hours for shop assistants. At one stage it claimed a readership of 40,000 people.

RAINEY: So ye're here at last, are ye? Kapin' the tay waitin'!

TOM: Och, sure, A cudden help it. A wus wi' Hughie!

RAINEY: Aye, ye're sure t'be late if ye're wi' him. Where's he?

TOM: A left him in Royal Avenue talkin' to Michael O'Hara.

RAINEY: What, thon Papish fella?

TOM: Aye, they went intil the Sinn Feiners' Hall thegither. *[He sits down and takes off his boots.]* He'll not be long. *[He takes off his coat and loosens his waistcoat.]*

RAINEY: A don't like Hughie goin' after Papishes. He knows a quare lock o' them.

MRS. RAINEY: Och, now, what harm is there in that. A'm sure Micky O'Hara's as nice a wee fella as ye cud wish t' meet.

RAINEY: Aw, A've nathin' agenst him, but A don't like Cathliks an' Prodesans mixin' thegither. No good ivir comes o' the like o' that.

[Tom goes into the scullery where the splashing noise is renewed.]

MRS. RAINEY: They'll have to mix in heaven, John.

RAINEY: This isn't heaven.

MRS. RAINEY: Indeed, that's true. What wi' stracks an' one thing an' another, it might be hell.

RAINEY: There's no peace where Catholiks an' Prodesans gits mixed up thegither. Luk at the way the Cathliks carry on on the Twelfth o' July. Ye have t' have the peelers houlin' them back for fear they'd make a riot. D'ye call that respectable or dacent?

MRS. RAINEY: Well, God knows, they git plenty of provokin'. What wi' them men that prache at the Custom House Steps an' yer or'nge arches an' the way the *Tellygraph* is always goin' on at them, A wonder they don't do more nor they do.

RAINEY: Aw, ye wur always one fur Cathliks!

MRS. RAINEY: A belave in lavin' people alone. Come on, an' have yer tay fur dear sake. Sure ye'd go on talkin' fur a lifetime if A wus to let ye.

St J. G. Ervine, *Mixed marriage* included in *Four Irish plays* (London, 1914), p.3.

Right: *Mountpottinger crossroads, East Belfast, close to where St J. Ervine lived (Green Collection, Ulster Folk Museum)*

Far right: *The Newtownards Road, East Belfast (Green Collection, Ulster Folk Museum)*

AROUND THE PROVINCE

A 1913 luxury tour, by charabanc, (Welch Collection, Ulster Museum)

Driving for the Tennis Hole, Ladies Course, Ballycastle, Co. Antrim (Welch Collection, Ulster Museum)

DELINA appeared just now on the platform, deeply moved at the blending masses who rushed at the last moment to catch the boat train.

With a warm hand-shake Lord Gifford bade his railway friend adieu, and conducted Delina to a gorgeous saloon that stood in readiness to convey them to their verdant destination. Its springy seats of all sizes, colour, and form, upholstered in velvet of richest make, imparted to their bodies the ease they craved, and caused Delina, whilst lying buried in sinking silence, to cast her thoughts on the immediate past into the near tide along which she was so closely and swiftly driven. Only forty minutes did they enjoy their room of refinement.

A first class saloon car (Welch Collection, Ulster Museum)

As the train slowly puffed into Larne Harbour station Delina suddenly jumped to her feet, and became pale as milk.

"What's the matter, dear?" spake Lord Gifford, rising hurriedly to his feet. "Is there anything wrong?"

"Oh, everything," she gasped, in despair, "for I've forgotten my little bundle. I left it in the waiting-room above."

"Bosh, child; what about it! Far nicer things, I presume, will await you once we are safely landed on the other side."

"But—but—I'd love to have it. My brooch is in it, and two embroidered handkerchiefs my mother gave me years ago, besides other wee things I've learned to love."

As there was little time to be lost, and to satisfy her wish, meagre as it was, Lord Gifford resolved to let her have it. He beckoned on the station-agent—now that the train had arrived at a standstill—whose genial manner and exemplary courteousness are widely known, and stated the case to him. Lord Gifford then gave him his card, making the necessary alterations in his address and asked that it be forwarded immediately.

Stroking his long, soft beard, that once claimed to be more gingered in colour, the station-agent answered him gently, yet assuredly, with the words, "Certainly so; it will have every attention."

Shortly afterwards, they were so steadily and quietly guided along from Larne Harbour and its fine, deep lough, above the shimmering and flashy waves of moonlit quash, that before they got completely free from viewing past possibilities, they were standing on Stranraer Harbour.

The quick despatch of business occasioned quicker despatch of trains. Before they found time to decide whether or not to proceed direct to London, the train steamed away, and soon stole from their view.

A fine hotel, however, came to their rescue. A peep into the supper-room showed the half-frightened maid tall ferns shedding a fanciful shade upon the neatly arranged flowers that decked the long table's snowy cover; hospitality, be it said, peeped from its very mirrors; the fruits of the earth, the fish of the sea, the fowls of the air, and the flesh of beasts, were nimbly sitting in their glass, china, and silver dishes, crushing, apparently, the table's face with their tempting delicacies. Around this well-lighted room sat many a jolly rover, inhaling the heated perfume of rosy Bacchus, and sniffing contentedly at the delightful combined odour of the huge supper-table. Further along oozed the fragrant scent of a Chinese plant, that mixed refreshingly with the fainter, more ethereal odour of the exquisite flowers, whose faces stood elegantly daubed, some deep, others deeper, with natural paints of every conceivable natural shade, and whose delightful differences of tint grew more faint as the night advanced; while the cheery click of china pleasantly greeted the ear, as the hungry fingers of a travelling throng craved to touch it.

Partaking heartily of a well-cooked supper, sleep soon found purchasers in Lord Gifford and Delina Delaney.

A. McK. Ros, *Delina Delaney*, (Belfast, 1898; 2nd ed., London, 1935), pp 72-5.

Amanda McKittrick Ros was without doubt the most eccentric Ulster writer of her day. Born near Drumaness, Co. Down, in 1860, she trained as a teacher and went to Larne where she married Andrew Ross, the local stationmaster (he is mentioned in this extract). As a writer she has been variously described. On the one hand she has been called the world's worst novelist and on the other a sort of literary 'Grandma Moses'. The latter description is clearly the fairer one. Completely lacking in literary sophistication, she wrote the most extraordinary and delightful prose. She was the authoress of *Delina Delaney* and of two other novels, *Irene Iddlesleigh* (Belfast, 1897), and *Helen Huddleson* (London, 1969); this last book was completed by Jack Loudan after her death. She also wrote poetry, including *Poems of puncture* (London, 1912) and *Fumes of formation* (Belfast, 1933). These works contain many references to her pet hates - lawyers and literary critics - one unfortunate lawyer who crossed her path was lampooned with the name Mickey Monkeyface McBlear. Her admirers formed clubs which met to exchange quotations from her writings; members of these clubs included Lord Beveridge, E. V. Lucas and Lord Oxford. She died in 1939. A good biography of her has been written by Jack Loudan-*O rare Amanda* (London, 1954; 2nd ed., 1969).

Dining room in the Slieve Donard Hotel, Newcastle, Co. Down (Lawrence Collection, National Library of Ireland)

UNDER THE GRASS

Where those green mounds o'erlook the mingling Erne
    And salt Atlantic, clay that walked as Man
A thousand years ago, some Vik-ing stern,
    May rest, or nameless Chieftain of the Clan;
And when my dusty remnant shall return
    To the great passive World, and nothing can
With eye, or lip, or finger, any more,
    O lay it there too, by the river shore.

The silver salmon shooting up the fall,
    Itself at once the arrow and the bow;
The shadow of the old quay's weedy wall
    Cast on the shining turbulence below;
The water-voice which ever seems to call
    Far off out of my childhood's long-ago;
The gentle washing of the harbour wave;
    Be these the sights and sounds around my grave.

Soothed also with thy friendly beck, my town,
    And near the square gray tower within whose shade
Was many of my kin's last lying down;
    Whilst, by the broad heavens changefully arrayed,
Empurpling mountains its horizon crown;
    And westward 'tween low hummocks is displayed,
In lightsome hours, the level pale blue sea,
    With sails upon it creeping silently:

Or, other time, beyond that tawny sand,
    An ocean glooming underneath the shroud
Drawn thick athwart it by tempestuous hand;
    When like a mighty fire the bar roars loud,
As though the whole sea came to whelm the land—
    The gull flies white against the stormy cloud,
And in the weather-gleam the breakers mark
    A ghastly line upon the waters dark.

A green unfading quilt above be spread,
    And freely round let all the breezes blow:
May children play beside the breathless bed,
    Holiday lasses by the cliff-edge go;
And manly games upon the sward be sped,
    And cheerful boats beneath the headland row;
And be the thought, if any rise, of me,
    What happy soul might wish that thought to be.

William Allingham, *Irish songs and poems* (London, 1887), pp 123-4.

This rather sombre poem was written by William Allingham in his last years as he contemplated death. After Ferguson, Allingham is undoubtedly the greatest poet in this anthology. The town referred to in the poem is of course Ballyshannon, Co. Donegal, where he was born in 1824. Educated at Ballyshannon he spent much of his early life in the north of Ireland while serving in the bank and the customs service. He became a close friend of Tennyson and was associated with members of the pre-Raphaelite group. After 1863 he lived permanently in England, returning only for brief periods to Ireland. From 1874-9 he was editor of *Fraser's Magazine*. Throughout his writing his upbringing remained a constant influence. Perhaps his best work was *Laurence Bloomfield*, published in book form in 1864. Consisting of twelve chapters of verse it was a powerful commentary on social conditions in the Irish countryside. Allingham wrote several other books of poetry containing famous poems of his such as 'The winding banks of Erne' and that well known poem 'The fairies'. He also wrote a play *Ashby Manor* (London, 1883). He died in 1889. For a good selection of his work see *William Allingham, an introduction* (Dublin, 1971) by Professor Alan Warner, and John Hewitt's, *The poems of William Allingham* (Dublin, 1967).

An open air auction scene in Portadown, Co. Armagh, about 1885. (Sprott Collection, Portadown College)

The pope at Killybuck is a comedy, the main theme of which is Orange-Green rivalry over land. This extract is from an auction scene. It was first performed at Ballycastle, Co. Antrim, in 1915 by the Dalriada Players who were one of a number of flourishing amateur dramatic societies to be found around the countryside at the time. When put on commercially in Belfast in 1917 its title was changed to *The auction at Killybuck* for fear that the original title would cause a riot. But in fact from its first production the play has greatly amused audiences throughout Ulster. Its author was Louis Joseph Walsh, a solicitor, born at Maghera, Co. Londonderry. After practising for a time in Co. Londonderry he served as a district justice in Co. Donegal. As well he was the author of a number of humorous plays and stories, mainly set in Ulster. Among these plays are *The guileless Saxon: an Ulster comedy in three acts* (Dublin, 1917), and *Equity follow the law* (Belfast, 1935). His collections of short stories include *Yarns of a country attorney: stories and sketches of life in rural Ulster* (Dublin, 1918). He was also the author of *On my keeping and theirs: a record of experiences 'on the run' in Derry gaol and Ballykinlar internment camp* (Dublin, 1921). Walsh died in 1942.

[Job Wilson and William John consult for a moment with much head-shaking, whilst the auctioneer keeps repeating "Going at the biddin' of £460. Any advance?"]

WILLIAM JOHN: £465.

ALEX: What do you say now, Mr. Convery? Will I put you down for £475?

[Dominick appears to hesitate.]

ALEX: Come on, man, a ten poun' note never raired ye, and before I wud let wan o' these black-nebbed, sour-faced Prisbyterians into a place I wanted, I wud either have it myself or I wud make the man that bought it over my head pay dear for it.

DOM: All right, I'ill give ye £475.

ALEX: Come on, William John. Is it £485? Nivir let it be sayed that a Papish put the cowe on ye. We bate them at Derry, Aughrim, and the Boyne; and we'ill bate them the day too. I wud allow no man that wus n't the right soort to own a fut o' lan' in oul' Killybuck.

[William John and Job again consult]

WILLIAM JOHN [feebly] : £480.

ALEX: £480 now offered. Any advance? Speak out, Dominick. The Swaterban blood was always plucky, and I hope you won't let a Prisbyterian get the better o' you for the sake of a wheen o' poun's.

DOM: Well, I suppose I may offer you £485; but I'm thinkin' it's me last bid.

ALEX: Now, Mr. Wilson, send forward the hosts of Israel. Where's the use o' talkin' again' the Home Rule Bill, if you let a five or ten poun' note keep ye from savin' Killybuck from all the horrors o' Popery, brass money and wooden shoes. Come, William John. Nivir say: "Die."

WILLIAM JOHN: I'ill give you another ten shillings.

ALEX: I cannot take any smaller bids that £5. Do you say £490?

WILLIAM JOHN *[after much nudging from Job, and as if he were expressing his consent to the amputation of his two legs]* : £490.

ALEX: £490 now offered. Any advance?

DOM: £495.

ALEX: Make it £500, William John.

WILLIAM JOHN: Naw, naw! It's over dear as it is, an' I went agin' me mind goin' this far.

L. J. Walsh, *The pope at Killybuck* (Dublin, 1915), p. 22

A COUNTRY LAD'S OBSERVATIONS AT THE
HIRING FAIR IN BALLYMENA.

Weel, freens, A gat me tae the toon,
Although big clouds were hoverin' roon,
An whiles an odd yin did come doon
    Tae we got drack'd;
Yet mony a sinburnt-luckin' croon
    Seem'd tae be cracked.

The hale toon seemed tae be aware
That Sethurday was Hiring Fair,
And that ferm-servants wud be there
    For a big day,
Who meant tae hae a treat sae rare
    Wae six months' pay.

Here and there wus a wee ban'
The centre-piece a big ould man,
What mak's his leevin' off the lan'
    Without a doot;

Bit see him view the horny han'
    'Ere he spak' oot.

"Tell me, my man, noo can you sow,
And can you milk, and plough, and mow,
And build a load of hay or stro'
    For market day?
If you can do these things, say so
    I'll fix your pay."

The toon assumed its usual gait,
Folk mashing roon at nae wee rate,
Each lucking' for their ain dear mate
    In blank despair;
And so may I if I keep blate
    To the next Fair.

November, 1899.

Adam Lynn, *Random rhymes from Cullybackey* (Belfast, 1911), pp 13-14.

Adam Lynn was born at Cullybackey, Co. Antrim, and worked in the linen industry. He wrote poetry for local papers such as the *Ballymena Observer*. During this period many newspapers had regular poetry columns and also published extracts from novels by popular authors. Writing in his local dialect, Lynn dealt with subjects like the Cullybackey cycling club, 'the twelfth', and the river Maine. No other works of his appear to have been published in book form.

Left: *Carrickmacross fair, Co. Monaghan (Lawrence Collection, National Library of Ireland)*

Right: *Customers at a fair in Portadown, Co. Armagh, about 1892 (Sprott Collection, Portadown College)*

Below: *Lending a hand in Castlewellan, Co. Down (Green Collection, Ulster Folk Museum)*

HE was gone without waiting for an answer, and in a few minutes was driving along the road in a small, light tax-cart.

Having driven about a mile up and down hill, he descried in the still lurid semi-darkness a little, broken-down vehicle standing outside a cabin-door, through which shone the glow of burning turf.

"Hum! I thought there was a break-down," he said. "I guessed how it would be when I heard Batt had sold her the broken-kneed pony." And, calling an urchin to hold his horse, he walked up the stone causeway to the cabin-door.

There he paused a moment, raised his hat and passed his hand over his forehead, frowned, and stepped over the threshold.

Bawn did not hear what was said; she was talking to the child, and the master of Tor had advanced and was standing beside her before she looked up. The gentleman stood observing her with a strange look on his face, noting her fair, smooth brow, her fresh, symmetrical cheeks, her laughing lips and eyes. In her black serge dress and shawl of shepherd's plaid she was exactly the same Bawn who had wrestled for her liberty with Somerled on board the steamer.

Bawn was sitting on a "creepy" stool before the blazing turf, her hat had been taken off, and her golden head was shining in the ruddy light. A bare-footed child was standing before her, finger in mouth, staring with fascinated eyes at the beautiful stranger, greatly to the delight of an aged man who sat shaking his head in the chimney-corner. Two sturdy men in sou'wester hats were directing Andy where to go for the loan of a little car to carry his mistress further, and a decent-looking woman was taking oat-cakes from a "griddle."

"But, sure, here's Misther Rory himself. Never fear but the masther'll pull ye out of the hobble."

She looked up with an unconscious, unexpecting smile, and saw the identical Somerled standing before her.

The smile died on her lips; the colour went out of

her cheeks; she rose and drew back a step, and looked him in the face. Impulsively trying to speak, her ready tongue was for once at fault. She drew her shawl around her, and met his eye defiantly.

Rosa Mulholland, *A fair emigrant* (London, 1888), pp 207-8.

Rosa Mulholland, born in Belfast in 1841, the daughter of a local doctor, was the authoress of many popular novels and books of poetry. She married John (later Sir John) Gilbert the antiquarian and deputy keeper of the public records in Dublin. Dickens encouraged her early work and published some of her short stories in *Household Words*. Her novels include *Marcella Grace* (London, 1886), and *The wild birds of Killeevy* (London, 1883). She died in 1921. About this time there were a number of Ulster women novelists writing books of a popular and sentimental nature: among others were M. T. Pender and M. de la C. Crommelin. The works of these writers were serialized in newspapers all over the country and undoubtedly influenced public opinion with their views, often telling, directly or indirectly, of Ireland's woes or England's glories.

Above: *In coastal areas where building stone was scarce cottages were sometimes made of turf sods, like this one at Magilligan, Co. Londonderry. Such a structure did not allow windows. (Welch Collection, Ulster Museum)*

Right: *A domestic scene (Rose Shaw Collection, Ulster Folk Museum)*

Thomas Caulfield Irwin, born in 1823 at Warrenpoint, Co. Down, was educated privately and in his youth travelled to Europe and north Africa. The family fortunes seem to have collapsed around 1848 and from that time on he appears to have been frequently impoverished. In later years he became eccentric, and even mad at times. From 1848 he contributed verse to many magazines, including the *Dublin University Review;* his writing was often of a high standard. His books of poetry include *Poems* (Dublin, 1866), and *Poems, sketches and songs* (Dublin, 1889). He also wrote a series of prose sketches, *Winter and summer stories* (Dublin, 1879). A good selection of Irwin's work can be found in *Irish poets of the nineteenth century*, (London, 1951), edited by Geoffrey Taylor. He died in Dublin in 1892.

SONNET

A roadside inn this summer Saturday:-
The doors are open to the wide warm air,
The parlour, whose old window views the bay,
Garnished with cracked delph full of flowers fair
From the fields round, and whence you see the glare
Fall heavy on the hot slate roofs and o'er
The wall's tree shadows drooping in the sun.
Now rambles slowly down the dusty street
The lazy drover's clattering cart; and crows
Fainter through afternoon the cock; with hoes
Tan faced harvest folk trudge in the heat:
The neighbours at their shady doors swept clean,
Gossip, and with cool eve fresh scents of wheat,
Grasses and leaves, come from the meadows green.

T. C. Irwin, *Versicles* (Dublin, 1883), p.45.

Far left: *Weary harvester enjoying her meal of potatoes and buttermilk (Green Collection, Ulster Folk Museum)*

Below: *Crosskey Inn, a former stage coach inn at Toome, Co. Antrim. (Green Collection, Ulster Folk Museum)*

JOHN [He looks at her, and then begins in a bashful manner]: You weren't at Ballyannis School fete; Sarah?

SARAH: No. But I heard you were there. Why?

JOHN [coming still closer]: I was expecting to see you.

SARAH [contemptuously]: I don't believe in young girls going to them things.

JOHN [gazing at her in astonishment]: But God bless me, they wouldn't call you young! [SARAH turns up her nose disgustedly.] I missed you. Man, I was looking for you all roads.

SARAH: I'm not a fool sort of young girl that you can just pass as idle hour or two with, John Murray, mind that.

JOHN: I never thought that of you, Sarah.

SARAH: Some people think that.

JOHN [astonished]: No.

SARAH: They do. There's Andy just after warning me this morning about making a fool of myself.

JOHN [puzzled]: But you never done that, Sarah.

SARAH: Well, he was just after giving me advice about going round flirting with Tom, Dick and Harry.

JOHN: Ah no, You never done that. Sure I knowed you this years and years, and you never had a boy to my knowing.

SARAH [offended]: Well I had, plenty. Only I just wouldn't take them. I refused more than three offers in my time.

JOHN [incredulously]: Well! Well! And you wouldn't have them!

SARAH: No.

JOHN: Why now?

SARAH (looking at him meaningly]: Well—I liked somebody else better.

JOHN [piqued]: Did he—the somebody—did he never ask you?

SARAH: He might yet, maybe.

JOHN [hopelessly to himself]: I wonder would it be any use then me asking her.

SARAH: And I'm beginning to think he is a long time thinking about it. [Knocking at the door.]

JOHN [angrily]: Ach! Who's that?

BROWN [opening yard door and looking in]: Me, sir. Mr. Dan wants to know could you not come out a minute, and show the gentleman what way you can stop the feedboard working.

JOHN: Don't you know yourself, you stupid headed lump you. Away back at once.

Rutherford Mayne, *The drone*, from *The drone and other plays* (Dublin, 1912), pp 27-9.

Above right: *Flower show at Sion Mills, Co. Tyrone, 1910 (Cooper Collection, Public Record Office of Northern Ireland)*

Right: *Take your partners! At the Foresters hall, Strabane, Co. Tyrone (Cooper Collection, Public Record Office of Northern Ireland)*

Rutherford Mayne was the pen-name of Samuel Waddell. Born in Japan in 1878, but brought up in Belfast, he joined the Ulster Literary Theatre in 1904, first as an actor and then as a playwright. His earliest play, *Turn of the road*, was performed by them in 1906. This was followed in 1908 by *The drone*, probably his most famous play, and one which has been performed in many countries since. These plays along with two others done at this time were published in 1912 (see above). Between 1912 and 1923 other works of his were staged by the Ulster Theatre group and the Abbey Theatre, but unfortunately they were not published. Like his earlier plays these were usually set in the Ulster countryside. Two later published works were *Bridge head* (London, 1939) and *Peter* (Dublin, 1944). He died in 1967.

His sister, Helen Waddell, was also a noted writer.

The main literary activity in Irish during this period in Ulster took the form of the collection of orally preserved material. People such as J. H. Lloyd, Rev. Lawrence Murray and Enrí Ó Muirgheasa, stimulated by the renewal of scholarly interest in Irish which occurred in these years (Eoin MacNeill and George Sigerson were two prominent Ulster figures in the new scholarship), set about gathering Irish poems and songs from the Ulster countryside. As well as *Céad de cheoltaibh Uladh*, Enri O Muirgheasa was responsible for another book of collected Ulster Gaelic poetry, *Dhá chéad de cheoltaibh Uladh* (Dublin, 1934). The above poem is a love song which came from Mairéad nic Mhuircheartaigh, an inhabitant of Rathlin Island, Co. Antrim. The poem is an interesting example of Rathlin dialect in which the vocabulary and idiom have pronounced Scots Gaelic characteristics. By 1885 a considerable number of people in Ulster still spoke Irish. This was especially so in north-west Donegal which has remained to this day one of the chief Irish speaking areas in Ireland.

Paddy the cliff climber, Rathlin Island, Co. Antrim — a well known local personality (Welch Collection, Ulster Museum).

MO MHÁIRE ÓG *(A Rathlin Song.)*

D'éaluigh m'athair 's d'éag mo mháthair,
  Is chan fheil mo cháirdean le fághail;
Acht cad atá mé gan crodh gan toigh,
  A bheith in dtóir ar Mháire Óig.

  Luinneóg.
Hó-ró-ró 's gur thú mo rún,
Thug me an gaol, 's cha b'aithreach liom,
Do'n nighin úd an chúil dualaigh dhuinn,
Is gur teith liom fhéin mo Mháire Óg.

Chan fheil duine uasal ó nó barún,
  Nó fear óg anns na fearann,
Nach bhfeil dúil aca le bainis,
  Ach chuile fhear, le Máire Óig.

Chan fheil duine 'sa ghleann úd thall—
  Eadar bun 's bárr a' ghleann'—
Nach bhfeil ag bagairt ar mo cheann
  Ar son a bheith in dtóir ar Mháire Óig.

Acht ná cuireadh sin ort-sa brón
  Fad is bhéas mo chuideacht beo
Congbhóchaidh mise duit-se an lón,
  Is má bha scór ann gheobhaidh sin dram.

Anonymous

Enrí Ó Muirgheasa, *Céad de cheoltaibh Uladh,* (Dublin,
1915), p. 101.

SHE was a stout, plain, ruddy-faced woman, and she was standing in her kitchen—the kitchen of the gardener's lodge—with a big apron covering the front of her striped cotton dress, and her sleeves rolled back from bare strong arms which, like her rough hands, were flaked with flour, for she was baking. The boy did not resemble her. He was slender, while she was stout; he was fine, while she was coarse; he seemed subtle, while she was simple; and there was an enigmatic expression in his dark, narrow, wide-set eyes—something half-mocking, half-ironic—which now and then made her feel vaguely uneasy. Subtle—and with little of that air of engaging innocence one expects of rustic youth. Brown-skinned, attractive, yet not quite agreeable. Her only child probably, her only son at all events—that could be gathered from the way she looked at him as she bent down to kiss him with a certain superficial roughness.

They lived—she and the boy and the boy's father— in the front lodge of the demesne, within sight and sound of the sea—and she came to the gate to see him off, watching his slender figure on the white, dusty, sunlit road as long as it remained in sight. At the curve of the road he looked back and waved his hand. He never forgot to do that; he knew it pleased her; and for that matter he never forgot anything. She waved too, but she returned to her baking with a sigh. She couldn't have told you

why she sighed, except that she wished she knew a little more about him; and there was nobody—least of all his taciturn unnoticing father—to whom she could express what she felt. She could not clearly express it to herself. She sometimes wondered if he would be a successful man, but more frequently, and with vague misgivings she was ashamed of, she hoped he would be a good one. For he *was* a good boy—always considerate and—and discreet. That was a very queer word to use. She did not like it, and did not know why she had used it. In any case, he would not be a gardener like his father, for he was clever. Mr. Connell had said that he ought to go to college, and that with scholarships it might be managed. He was now nearly fifteen and still at the village school. But in her day-dreams she already saw him, after a brilliant University career, returning home, stiffly garbed in black, assistant and successor to the present minister.

Forrest Reid, *Retrospective adventures* (London, 1941), pp 221-1.

Left: *Three Walker brothers, Belfast, 1892. From right to left: Thomas, who became a Presbyterian minister, James, a Church of Ireland curate, and Carlisle, who, amongst other things became grandfather of the author!* (author's collection)

Far left: *A gate lodge of Belvoir estate, Knockbreda, Co. Down, home of Lord Deramore* (author's collection)

This extract is from a short story 'The accomplice,' written in 1913 and first published in 1917. The author, Forrest Reid (1876-1947), was born in Belfast and spent most of his life there. He was responsible for a number of important novels including *Uncle Stephen* (London, 1931), *Brian Westby* (London, 1934), *The retreat* (London, 1936), *Uncle Tom* (London, 1944) and *Peter Waring* (London, 1937). He also wrote two interesting volumes of autobiography, *Apostate* (London, 1926), and *Private road* (London, 1940); the first of these contains a vivid portrait of life in Victorian Belfast. A contributor to the magazine *Uladh*, Reid wrote articles for many other magazines including the *Westminster Review* and the *Ulster Review*. In addition he reviewed books for the *Manchester Guardian*, an occupation which for some time was his only source of income. He was a close friend of E. M. Forster, and other important contemporary English writers. In 1953 a critical study of his work was written by Russell Burlingham, *Forrest Reid, a portrait and a study* (London, 1953).

THE CIRCUS

THE circus! what a brilliant sight!
    Fine horsemanship was there, sir;
Fine ladies, too, rode round the ring,
    Of clothing somewhat bare, sir.
These boldly dashed through paper hoops,
    Displaying feats of daring;
And posed in many a curious way
    To keep the youngsters staring.

One man could play with glittering knives
    As though they were but toys, sir;
Another one could fling like balls
    Two handsome little boys, sir.
My friends were much amused to see
    The "dwarf" at big men rushing;
But ah, those ladies, semi-clad—
    They kept some females blushing!

Their "afterpiece" was but a sham,
    Unworthy to be seen, sir;
They must have thought their audience here
    Was truly very green, sir.
But when they come to town again,
    They surely must display less
Of female charms. or, much I fear,
    Some female friends will pay less.

J. W. Montgomery, *Fireside lyrics* (Downpatrick, 1887), pp 59-60.

Above left: *Mr. John Duffy, of the famous Duffy's circus, and friend, Strabane, Co. Tyrone (Cooper Collection, Public Record Office of Northern Ireland)*

Above right: *Perhaps like some of those naughty dancers mentioned above — Buff Bill's Dixie Girls, Strabane, 1910! (Cooper Collection, Public Record Office of Northern Ireland)*

Right: *Young spectators at a Punch'n Judy show, Doagh, Co. Antrim (author's collection)*

Known as the Bard of Bailieborough, John Wilson Montgomery was a native of Virginia, Co. Cavan. He spent some years as master of the workhouse at Bailieborough but the greater part of his life was spent in Downpatrick, Co. Down, where he was clerk to the poor law board of guardians. He was an enthusiastic antiquarian, frequently writing pieces on local antiquities for newspapers. His best literary work was probably his first volume of poems, *Rhymes Ulidian* (Downpatrick, 1877). In addition to this and *Fireside lyrics*, he wrote a small volume of prose sketches, *Round Mourne* (Bangor, 1908). He died in 1911 at the age of 76.

T was just in the middle av Ballygullion sthreet I met Billy av the Hills, the last man in life I thought to meet there on a market-day. In his spare time Billy does be makin' an odd dhrop av potheen; an' the market-day bein' a throng day for the polis in Ballygullion, 'twas ginerally Billy's throng day outside av it, deliverin' a wee keg here an' there.

"You're a sight for sore eyes, Billy," sez I. "What has fetched ye intil the town the day?"

"Ye know ould Dick Taafe, me uncle be marriage," sez Billy. "His brother's dead, away in Donegal, an' he's goin' off to the funeral in the mornin'. I'm sleepin' in the house a night or two to keep the aunt company, an' I come in the day to rise me uncle in good time for the thrain; for he's desperate heavy-headed, and the aunt's little betther, though she wouldn't give in till it. Come on down an' have a crack before ye go home."

So away we goes down to the house, an' whin we got that length, who should be there wi' Mrs. Taafe but wee Jinks, the pedlar,—Peddlin' Tam as they call him,—wi' a whole packful av stuff spread out on the table.

"Good-evenin', gintlemen," sez he. "Ye might come an' give me a hand. I'm just thryin' to sell the misthress here the very thing she wants."

"What's that?" sez Billy. "It'll be somethin' in the way av clothes, I'm thinkin'."

"Not a bit av it," sez the pedlar, "it's just an alarm clock. Sure her heart's broke wi' wakin' the man in the mornin's; an' this is the boy'll do it for her."

"I don't believe in thim conthrivances," sez she; "ye could niver depend on thim."

"Hould on till I show ye how she works," sez Tam, "an' then ye'll change your mind. She's set for five," sez he; "now listen till her ringin', for it's herself can do it."

"Ay, there ye are now," sez the aunt. "Sure it's seven o'clock now, an' she'd be ringin' two hours slow. That'd be a dale av use in the mornin'."

"But ye can set her for any time ye like," sez Tam. "Wait a minit an' I'll set her to seven."

"An' mightn't ye as well get up to raise the house as get up to set the clock to do it," sez she. "It bates me to see the use av it at all."

I wish ye'd seen the pedlar's face. 'Twas little compliment to the ould woman's brains was in the back av his head, I'm thinkin'.

Lynn Doyle, *Ballygullion* (Dublin, 1908), pp 98-100.

Left: Market day in Lisburn, Co. Antrim (Green Collection, Ulster Folk Museum)
Below: O'Donnell's wine and spirit store, Lifford, Co. Donegal. Mr. Hugh O'Donnell, the proprietor, is standing in the centre (Cooper Collection, Public Record Office of Northern Ireland)

Lynn Doyle was the pseudonym of Leslie Alexander Montgomery. Born near Downpatrick, Co. Down, in 1873, he was the author of a number of plays staged by the Ulster Literary Theatre. These include *The lilac ribbon, The turncoats* and *Love and land.* However, Lynn Doyle is best remembered for his humorous stories about the imaginary Ulster district of Ballygullion and its people. They tell of fairs, poaching, politics and everyday events, all amusingly portrayed. The above extract is from a chapter called 'The alarm clock'. Later editions of the book were illustrated by William Conor. Other books on Ballygullion followed, including *Ballygullion ballads* (London, 1936). Doyle also wrote an autobiography, *An Ulster childhood* (Dublin, 1921). By profession he was a banker, serving as a branch manager at Cushendall, Co. Antrim, Keady, Co. Armagh, and Skerries, Co. Dublin. He died in 1961.

THE FLOWER OF MAGHERALLY

'Twas at a fair near Banbridge town
   I met this blooming maiden O;
Sure Adam was not more surprised
   When he first saw Eve in Eden O!

Her yellow hair in ringlets fair,
   Her shoes of Spanish leather O!
She is the girl that won my heart,
   And keeps it in the tether O!

And let them all say what they can,
   Or let them scoff or rally O!
She is the darlin' of my heart,
   An' the flower of Magherally O!

Journal of the Irish Folk Song Society,
(London, 1904; reprinted, 1967) vol. 12,
no. 2, pp 57-8.

Right: *Arriving in town (Sprott
Collection, Portadown College)*
Left: *Observers at the pig market in
Woodhouse Street, Portadown, about
1885 (Sprott Collection, Portadown
College)*

This folk song was recorded by a Miss Maud Houston who learnt it from a Mrs. Ryan, who in her turn heard it sung on a Belfast street by a ballad monger! During the period covered by this book, Maud Houston and others like Joseph Campbell, F. J. Bigger and Padric Gregory continued the work begun by Dr. George Petrie and Edward Bunting in collecting folk songs and music. Right up to the present day folk song is a living, active cultural tradition to be found throughout the Ulster countryside. These songs tell of many things — emigration, love, work, politics and important events. Some of the songs being sung at the turn of the century can be read in the journals of the Irish Folk Song Society in this period. More recently a collection of Ulster folk songs has been made by Robin Morton, *Folk songs sung in Ulster* (Cork, 1970)

THERE was no nonsense about the Alexanders. So the head of the family had been asserting so vehemently since he had built his house, calling it Ardreagh, that the shrewd ones among his hearers felt certain that there must have been a good deal of nonsense about the Alexanders, or he would not have been so urgent in his protestations to the contrary. But those who were the shrewdest knew perfectly well that all James Alexander meant by his protestations was that he would not alter his dinner hour from one o'clock to half-past seven, though he could well afford to do so, in imitation of the gentry, and that he would not "set up" a butler or a footman as several ostentatious families whom he could name had done as soon as they had got on a bit in the world, or even sooner.

"We began life as plain people and we intend to remain plain people," he said when his neighbours had rallied him in the unambiguous way they adopt in the North of Ireland when they wish to be satirical, about the building of the house. "Late dinner, swallow-tail coat and white choker? No fears! Many's the time I've eat my dinner in my shirt-sleeves, and felt nothing the worse for it, and many's the time I'll do it again if I've a mind to. And if I don't put on a white choker when I'm at my dinner, you may be sure that I'll have no man at the back of my chair with one round his neck. And them that that's not good enough for can stay away from my house."

This ostentatious unostentation deceived no one. Everyone knew that he was overflowing with pride at being able to build Ardreagh; and for having a dining-room four feet longer than the corresponding apartment in Danesfort, the mansion which Mr. Megarry of the Ballyboye Mills had built for himself, and the Megarrys were one of the old families in Ballyboye,

having held their mill since long before the Civil War in America set all the linen lappers in Belfast looking about to see where they could build a mill. Mr. Alexander had been one of the lads in the Megarrys' mill at Ballyboye.

"What's the length of thon room?" he had asked his architect when the plans of Ardreagh were laid before him, and he laid a finger upon the biggest of the squares outlined before him.

"Twenty-five feet, not including the bay window," replied the architect.

"And what's the size of the biggest room at Danesfort—you built Danesfort, didn't you?"

"Twenty-six feet, I believe."

"Then make mine thirty. I'll show them what I can do, though Megarry give me many's a clout on the ear when he looked into the carding-room, and him and me was one age."

The architect smiled.

"You've given him many a clout since, Mr. Alexander, by all accounts," said he.

"Ay, many's a one—many's a one; and this'll be another—make

it a good four feet longer. It'll be a brave wee clout that he'll feel when it gets abroad that Jimmy Alexander has built a dining-room in his new house more'n four feet longer nor the best Charlie Megarry could do with. I wouldn't keep it a secret if I was you; it may do you good in your business to let people know that you can build such a room."

"You may trust to me, Mr. Alexander, but I doubt if Mr. Megarry will feel it to be as sore a clout as your getting the big order for the Green Star sheets last year—a thousand dozen, wasn't it?" said the architect.

Mr. Alexander's eyes gleamed, his mouth twitched as it he were licking his lips.

"A clout? Yon was no clout, it was a dunch—man, but I hit him a quare dunch that day."

"It will be a long day before that thousand dozen sheets turn into clouts," remarked the architect.

And when he got back to his office in Belfast he gave a good imitation of his client's gloating over the prestige conferred upon him by the possession of a thirty-foot dining-room; and his partner, who was an adept at cubic measure as it related to the increasing of the dimensions of a room beyond the limits contracted for, took good care that Mr. Alexander paid fully for the luxury of "clouting" the man who had been severe to him in his youth forty years before.

And the people before whom Mr. Alexander protested himself to be a plain man and without any

Above: *An interior view of Derryvolgie house, South Belfast (Welch Collection, Ulster Museum)*

nonsense grinned and asked if it was true that Mr. Megarry was adding another ten feet to his dining-room. There is no great subtlety in the sarcasm of the North of Ireland business man.

F. F. Moore, *The Ulsterman, a story of today* (London, 1914), pp29-31.

Born at Limerick in 1855, Frank Frankfort Moore was brought up in Belfast where he was educated at the Royal Belfast Academical Institution. From 1876-92 he was on the reporting staff of the *Belfast News Letter*. He then moved to England where he spent the remainder of his life. His first major novel, *I forbid the banns*, published in 1893 in London, was extremely success-ful. Other novels include *The jessamy bride* (London, 1897) and *Castle Omeragh* (London, 1903). *The Ulster-man*, from which the above extract is taken, is set in the Ulster of the 1912-14 home-rule crisis period amongst a self-made linen family. As well at this time he was the author of *The truth about Ulster* (London, 1914). His novels were frequently serialized in magazines like *The Graphic* and *The Queen*. Moore also wrote a number of plays which were performed in London and Dublin. He died in 1931.

*Wrong turn — car in the canal basin, Strabane, Co. Tyrone, 1910
(Cooper Collection, Public Record Office of Northern Ireland)*

A motor cycle unit of the Ulster Volunteer Force, 1913 (Public Record Office of Northern Ireland)

Eviction scene in Co. Fermanagh, probably in the late 1880s (Lawrence Collection, National Library of Ireland)

VICTORY

West Belfast for Ireland!

My countymen, arise, rejoice,
   Democracy has won the day;
For West Belfast, in ringing voice,
   Proclaims against the tyrant sway.
Uplift your souls in joyful song,
   Attune your lyres to hymns of praise,
For Right has triumphed over Wrong,
   And numbered are Oppression's days.

Our Standard Bearer is returned
   To voice our sentiments again;
The people trampled on and spurned
   And shackled with vile slavery's chain,
Have risen boldly at the sound
   Of holy Freedom's clarion blast,
The foes of Progress to confound
   In staunch, unconquered West Belfast.

Upon the ramparts can be seen
   Our banner waving proudly still,
The Orange blending with the Green,
   New emblem of the people's will—
The people's will that reigns supreme
   In what concerns a nation's life—
Democracy's bold choice redeem
   From cruel, vain, religious strife.

Then let me grasp your Orange hand!
   I greet you as a patriot brother,
Let both work for our Fatherland,
   And mutual aid give to each other;
My foes are yours, and yours are mine,
   And we must fall or stand united;
Our native strength we must combine,
   Living no more as slaves benighted.

NO SURRENDER

Within the bounds of British sway
   Old Ireland clamours restlessly,
But come what will or come what may
   The Union rules her destiny.

Out in the cold with birthright sold,
   We dare not let her thus decline;
To Britons bold keep firm your hold
   Lest poverty of fate be thine.

Her rash desire our hearts inspire
   Old Erin's honour to maintain;
Vanish vampire! guard the Empire,
   That rules supreme the rolling main.

With equal laws in freedom's cause
   Proud "Britons never shall be slaves;"
A "Home Rule" clause in Union laws
   Dispelled shall be by loyal braves.

March forward, then, bold Ulster men,
   Resound your harp right manfully;
O'er hill and glen, o'er Shamrock stem
   Uphold the flag of UNITY—

Top right: *Joseph Devlin, Ulster Nationalist leader (Public Record Office of Northern Ireland)*
Top left: *Capt. James Craig, later Lord Craigavon, Ulster Unionist leader (Public Record Office of Northern Ireland)*
Bottom right: *William Walker, Ulster Labour leader*
Bottom left: *W. S. Armour, Ulster Liberal leader (J.K.C. Armour's private collection)*

These two examples of political doggerel date from the 1910 (Dec.) general election. The one on the right was printed in the *Northern Whig* 2 Dec., 1910, while the other on the left, celebrating Joe Devlin's victory in the December election, was printed on a broadsheet. This particular broadsheet came from the collection in the Belfast Central Library. Other interesting collections of ballad broadsheets can be found in Queen's University and the Ulster Folk Museum.

George A. Birmingham was the pseudonym of Canon James Owen Hannay. Born in 1865 at what is now 75 University Road, Belfast, Birmingham was an author of considerable ability and vast productivity. He wrote 44 novels, 3 plays, an opera libretto and 16 other books. The novel from which this extract is taken is set, like a number of his works, in the north. Although it was published in the middle of 1912, it tells of guns being brought secretly into ports and volunteers marching through the streets of Belfast: This was all very soon to happen. Some of his other novels are interesting portraits of the changing social scene in Ireland at the turn of the century, especially *The seething pot* (London, 1904), *Spanish gold* (London, 1908) and *The bad times* (London, 1907); this last book is set in the west of Ireland around the time of the land war in the early 1880s. Birmingham spent 21 years as rector in Westport, Co. Mayo. He left Westport in 1913 - partly because of objections from local people who thought themselves portrayed in one of his books. In 1924 he moved to England where he was rector of several parishes before his death in 1950.

Unionist clubs marching to Belfast City Hall to sign the Ulster covenant, opposing home-rule, 28 Sept. 1912 (Welch Collection, Ulster Museum)

T HE reading-room of the club is on the first floor, and the window commands an excellent view of Donegall Place, one of the principal thoroughfares of Belfast. The club stands right across the eastern end of the street, and the traffic is diverted to right and left along Royal Avenue and High Street. At the far, the western end, of Donegall Place, stands the new City Hall, with the statue of Queen Victoria in front of it. There again the traffic is split at right angles. Some of the best shops in the town lie on either side of this street. A continuous stream of trams passes up and down it, to and from the junction, which is directly under the club windows, and is the centre of the whole Belfast tramway system. It is always pleasant to stand at the reading-room window and watch the very busy and strenuous traffic of this street. As a view point on that particular morning the window was as good as possible. Donegall Place is the chief and most obvious way from the northern and eastern parts of the city to the place where the meeting was to be held.

Between eleven o'clock and twelve the volunteers began to appear in considerable numbers. I saw at once that I had been wrong in supposing that they meant to spend the day in bed. One company after another came up Royal Avenue or swung round the corner from High Street, and marched before my eyes along Donegall Place towards the scene of the meeting. Small bodies of police appeared here and there, heading in the same direction. Now and then a few mounted police trotted by, making nearly as much jangle as if they had been regular soldiers. The hour fixed for the meeting was one o'clock, but at noon the number of men in the street was so great that ordinary traffic was stopped. A long line of trams, unable to force their way along, blocked the centre of the thoroughfare. The drivers and conductors left them and went away. Crowds of women and children collected on the roofs of these trams and cheered the men as they marched along.

G. A. Birmingham, *The Red Hand of Ulster,* (London, July 1912; reprint Dublin, 1973), pp 242-3.

THOMPSON: I was promoted this year to be one of King William's Generals.

GRANIA: And you lead your fighting kerns into the heat of battle?

THOMPSON: *[confidently]* : Indeed, to tell you the truth, I never got the length of the field.

GRANIA: That is strange.

THOMPSON: I was takin' a short cut through the meadows, and while I was climbing a ditch, my ould gun burst in my hands, an' that is all I mind. I must a lay there all day and then maybe in the night I wandered about, not knowin' where I was, and then I must have fell asleep, and when I wakened up in the mornin' I didn't know where I was, and I'm damned if I know now—excuse me.

GRANIA: And you know not if your army was victorious or not?

THOMPSON: Sure I told you I was on King William's side. Of course we won the day.

GRANIA: Why do you say "of course"? The fortunes of war are so uncertain.

THOMPSON: Sure it wasn't a real fight. It was a sham fight or a pageant fight.

GRANIA: A make-believe. *[Thompson nods his head]*

THOMPSON: Aye, the very thing.

GRANIA: But *have* you been in a *real* fight?

THOMPSON: O aye, I was in a scrap in Portadown last Sunday.

GRANIA: And whom were you fighting in Portadown?

THOMPSON: The Hibernians.

GRANIA [shocked] : The Hiberniana! But are not all the people in Erinn Hibernians?

THOMPSON: In sowl they're not.

GRANIA: Are all the people in Portadown Hiberniana?

THOMPSON: Talk sense, woman dear.

GRANIA [looking towards audience] : Many changes must have come o'er Erinn since the days of Cuchulain and Oisin. Then we were all Hibernians. [To Thompson.] I wish dearest that you were an Hibernian too.

THOMPSON: You'll never see the day. [Rising from couch.] And what's more, I'll have nothing more to do with you, for I'm no believer in mixed marriages.

Gerald McNamara, *Thompson in Tir-na-n-Og* (Dublin, n.d.),p 24

Thompson in Tir-na-n-Og was first performed in 1912 at the Grand Opera House in Belfast. The play centres round an Orangeman, Thompson, who, after his gun blows up accidentally on his way to the Scarva field on the 13th of July, wakes up in the land of eternal youth, Tir-na-n-Og, peopled by Celtic gods and heroes. The scene which follows, where Orange and Hibernian views confront each other in a marvellous burlesque, has amused Ulster audiences ever since. Harry Morrow, the real name of the author, Gerald McNamara, was one of six very talented Morrow brothers who contributed much to the Ulster stage in the early part of the century. He was a founder member of the Ulster Literary Theatre, and was an actor as well as a playwright. His other plays, which unfortunately were mostly never published, include *Suzanne and the sovereigns*, *The throwbacks*, *No surrender* and *Who fears to speak?* Some of his sketches and short plays were, however, published in the *Dublin Magazine*. Born in 1866, he died in 1938.

Far left: *Twelfth platform, Strabane area, about 1912 (Cooper Collection, Public Record Office of Northern Ireland)*

Below: *Ancient Order of Hibernians, Cloughcorr, no. 463, in 1911 (Cooper Collection, Public Record Office of Northern Ireland)*

This extract is taken from a novel the first part of which is set in the Belfast of the1880s and 1890s. The attack described here is almost certainly based on the attack on the the Shankill Road R.I.C. barracks in the riots of 1886. James Douglas, author of *The unpardonable sin*, was born and brought up in Belfast. He moved to London where he worked as a journalist, becoming editor of the *Sunday Express* in 1920, a position he held for eleven years. His other writings include *Poems and songs of Robert Burns*, published in London in 1906, and *The man in the pulpit* (London, 1905). He died in 1940 at the age of 73.

aving his cap in the air, Andy dashed at the railings and seizing the spikes endeavoured to clamber over them. The crowd was suddenly stung to madness, and surged forward, hurling stones over Andy's head. Andy had one foot over the railings, and was about to drop into the garden, when he heard a man behind him cry out - 'Duck, boys, duck; they're going to fire.'

Lifting his eyes, he saw through the window three policemen dropping on their knees and raising their rifles to their shoulders. There was a blinding flash of flame and a noise like thunder, and Andy rolled off the railings into the garden in a tumbled heap.

But it was too late to check the onset of the infuriated mob. The railings collapsed under the weight of the impact of the solid mass. They

Left: *Shankill Road R.I.C. barracks after the attack on it, June 1886, in which eight people were killed. (Welch Collection, Ulster Museum)*

Right: *Funeral of victims of Belfast riots, 1907, at Dunville Park.*

poured through the window, and the barrack-room was filled with a confused press of combatants. The police defended themselves desperately, swinging their rifles by the barrel and dealing savage blows at the heads of their assailants as they appeared at the window. They fought behind a rampart of senseless bodies, but it was evident that the crowd would in the end break down their defence. The inspector realised that the situation was critical, and ordered six of his men to fire upon the crowd from the windows on the first floor.

'Give them buck-shot first' said he, 'and then ball if necessary.'

The six policemen fired simultaneously into the seething mass below. A roar of pain and rage burst forth, and in a mad panic the rioters broke and fled. The police fired a second round of buck-shot into the flying mass. Several of the running men stumbled and fell on the road, then dragged themselves to their feet and staggered into shelter. Some of them found refuge in side streets; others rushed into houses, the doors of which were opened by friendly hands. In a few moments the street was empty and silent; only a dark leaf remained in the garden under the broken railings.

The police were so deeply engrossed with the task of attending to their wounds, and to the wounds of the rioters who had been left behind, that they did not observe an old, grey-haired woman stealing softly towards the boy. She lifted him tenderly in her arms and carried him away.

James Douglas, *The unpardonable sin* (London, 1907), pp 132-4.

THE WATCHWORD

"Take and Hold."

O, hear ye the watchword of Labor.
  The slogan of they who'd be free,
That no more to any enslaver
  Must Labor bend suppliant knee.
That we on whose shoulders are borne
  The pomp and the pride of the great,
Whose toil they repaid with their scorn,
  Should meet it at last with our hate.

Chorus.

Then send it afar on the breeze, boys,
  That watchword, the grandest we've known,
That Labor must rise from its knees, boys,
  And take the broad earth as its own.

Aye, we who oft won by our valor,
  Empire for our rulers and lords,
Yet knelt in abasement and squalor
  To that we had made by our swords.
Now valor with worth will be blending,
  When, answering Labor's command,
We arise from the earth and ascending
  To manhood, for Freedom take stand.

Chorus.

Then out from the field and the city,
  From workshop, from mill and from mine,
Despising their wrath and their pity,
  We workers are moving in line.
To answer the watchword and token
Nor pause till our fetters we've broken,
  And conquered the spoiler and drone.

Chorus.

James Connolly, *Songs of freedom by Irish writers* (New York, 1907), p.3.

SCENES FROM BELFAST STRIKE 1907

Above: *Lorry overturned by strikers in Gt. George's Street.*
Top left: *Motor waggon and police escort in Donegall Street.*
Bottom left: *Maxim gun section of the Middlesex Regiment in Ormeau Park. (Linenhall Library)*

James Connolly was born in Edinburgh in 1868 of Irish parents. In 1895 he moved to Ireland and became a leading member of the Irish trade union and socialist movements. From 1911 to 1914 he was centred in Belfast. Most of his writing took the form of political and historical works but he was also the author of a number of poems including 'Hymn of freedom' and 'Freedom's sun'. As well he was the author of *Under which flag,* a three act play which was staged in 1916 in Liberty Hall, Dublin. The script of this play was lost until recently but in 1970 it was performed again in Dublin. In the 1916 Easter Rising in Dublin he took a leading role; for this action he was executed on May 12th. A new biography of him has recently been written by Samuel Levenson — *James Connolly, a biography* (London, 1973).

A hideous thought. I'll walk a while in the Park
And rid my mind of it. I wish to God
I had not said it: though no man can say
I counselled or advised it: only this;
I did not, as I ought, advise *against*—
Express some detestation—say, at least,
Such crimes are cowardly, and Irishmen,
Having the true faith, should be bold to act
The manlier part.
                    Yes, here I'm in the Park.

. . . .

        What's here? A fence of hurdles. Oh I see.
This is the Polo-Ground. But, what, what, what,
I'm here in Carey's footsteps!—Yes, 'twas here,
This very spot, I'm certain that he stood
Waiting,—foul images, I say begone!
Why should ye haunt my mind? What hand had I
In Carey's plot or Brady's butcherings?
I do detest them; and I ask myself
Pardon for words of question, where all's sure.
But, 'tis the mischief of such thoughts as these—
Of fire, assassination, dynamite—
One can't allow them entrance in the mind,
But straight the mind will turn to speculate
How this thing might be managed and how that,
And none the wiser. Carey thought himself
So safe, he laughed and puffed his cigarette
Leaving the prison van. Well, what he did
At last was right.
                    And what were right for me
To do at this conjuncture? Openly
Avow my sorrow that untimely words
Escaped me which some miscreant might wrest
To implication of assent to crime?
That were heroic, that were right indeed;
My conscience so inclines. I would not bear
The blame of giving entrance, thoughtlessly,

To wicked thoughts in other minds. For none
Amongst my hearers, thinking I approved,
But well might set his wits imagining
How he would carry on his private war
Were he Avenger: how he should procure
His stuffs; how keep a good face to the world;
And think it easy since a single man
Risking no more than his particular life.
With fairly even chances of escape,
Might carry half a town's destruction packed
In greatcoat-pockets or a Gladstone bag;
Or dowdy woman drop her petticoat
And wreck a nation's palace, and walk off
Slim and secure; or gleeful speculate
What were the outraged Briton's sentiments
And attitude regarding Ireland's right,
Should some fine morning show Westminster Bridge
Half discontinuous, or Victoria Tower
Hanging side-rent and ready to come down
Lengthwise along the roof of the House of Lords?
Or should some *quasi* city shopkeeper
Have tunnelled till he got below the Bank,
And sent the gold he scorned to touch sky-high
Far as the Strand? and think within himself
That Pharaoh, when he heard the mourning cry
For Egypt's first-born, were not more in haste
To let the Jews go than the Irish they.
        More I could fancy; but immoral thoughts
Fancied in others might infect myself
And that were what our guides in ethics call
Morosa delectatio, and a sin:
Sin's punishment, besides; for greater pain
Hardly attends the damned than have their minds
Compelled to dwell, whether they will or no,
On thoughts they know are evil. What to these
Were Carey's worst imaginings? Two or three
Men in high office, well-instructed men,
Who knew the perils that attend on place,

And, haply, were not wholly unprepared—
What these, compared with casual multitudes
Of young and old sent indiscriminate
To death and pain? Or what the finished Law
On those poor self-imagined Brutuses.
To rage of angered cities, when the arm
Of civil power is impotent to stay
A people's fury bent on massacre,
On bloody vengance, fire and banishment?
      Yes, here he waited till the man in grey
Should show himself approaching. Here his fate
Turned on the central pivot, once for all.
Had Carey, then, but walked the other way,
And meeting Under-secretary Burke,
Said, "Sir, I would not have you walk alone
Further, just now," it might have all been stopped,
And no blood spilt, and no necks stretched over there.
But here he stood, and had his chance, and chose
To walk in front and show the handkerchief:
And, in his pausing footsteps, here stand I
Still free to turn whichever way I will."

Sir Samuel Ferguson

Lady M. C. Ferguson, *Sir Samuel Ferguson in the Ireland of his day* vol. 1, (London, 1896), pp 263-7.
Written in early 1886, this poem was one of Sir Samuel Ferguson's last. In it he imagined himself following the steps of James Carey, one of the men who murdered chief-secretary Lord Frederick Cavendish and under-secretary T. H. Burke, May 1882, in Dublin's Phoenix Park.

Sir Samuel Ferguson (Royal Irish Academy)

Sir Samuel Ferguson was probably the most prominent Irish poet of the nineteenth century. Born in Belfast in 1810 he was educated at the Royal Belfast Academical Institution. After following a legal career until 1867 he became deputy-keeper of the public records of Ireland. In 1878 he was knighted for his work in reorganising the Irish records. From early days in Belfast he contributed verse to literary magazines including *Blackwoods*. Although most of his life was spent outside Ulster many of his poems call on the Ulster countryside and past: the ballad 'Anna Grace' is perhaps the best known of these. Ferguson developed a deep knowledge of early Irish legends and literature and his various long poems based on stories of the Irish past played an important role in the literary and cultural revival which occurred at the end of the century. For some this movement was to have nationalist overtones but not for Sir Samuel who, after a brief encounter with the repeal movement in the late 1840s became a strong believer in the union with Great Britain. He died in 1886. His wife, Lady Mary Catherine Ferguson, wrote a biography of him and it is from this that the poem on the other page is taken. Several collected editions of his work have been produced, the most recent being *Poems of Sir Samuel Ferguson* (Dublin, 1963), introduced by Padraic Colum.

The end of an era, Ulster affairs overshadowed by events in Europe — the outbreak of the First World War. This photograph shows soldiers of the 36th (Ulster) Division marching past through Donegall Square, Belfast, shortly before embarkation for France. (Public Record Office of Northern Ireland)

SELECT BIBLIOGRAPHY

HISTORICAL BACKGROUND
J. C. Beckett. *A short history of Ireland.* London, 1952. 5th edition, 1973.
J. C. Beckett. *The making of modern Ireland, 1603-1923.* London, 1966.
F. S. L. Lyons. *Ireland since the famine.* London, 1971.
T. W. Moody. *The Ulster question 1603-1973.* Cork, 1974.
T. W. Moody and J. C. Beckett (ed.). *Ulster since 1800.* 2 series: (1) *A political and economic survey;* (2) *A social survey.* London, 1955, 1957.
L. M. Cullen. *Six generations.* Cork, 1970.
A. T. Q. Stewart. *The Ulster Crisis.* London, 1967.
Belfast Telegraph. 1 Sept. 1970. This centenary edition of the paper has many excellent articles on Ulster life at the turn of the century.

FOLKLIFE
E. E. Evans. *Irish folk ways.* London, 1957. 4th impression, 1967.
E. E. Evans. *Mourne country: landscape and life in south Down.* Dundalk, 1951. 2nd revised edition, 1967.
Alan Gailey. *Irish folk drama.* Cork, 1969.
G. B. Adams (ed.) *Ulster dialects.* Holywood, Co. Down, 1964.
Ulster Folklife. Holywood, Co. Down, 1955-

WRITERS
R. J. Hayes (ed.) *Sources for the history of Irish civilization. Articles in Irish periodicals.* 10 vols. Boston (Mass.), 1970. This provides a guide to magazine articles on and by Ulster authors.
D. J. O'Donoghue. *The poets of Ireland.* Dublin, 1912. Reprint, New York, 1970.
S. J. Brown. *Ireland in fiction,* with introduction by D. J. Clarke, London, 2nd edition, 1919. Reprint, Shannon, 1968.
B. T. Cleeve. *Dictionary of Irish writers.* 3 series: (1) *Fiction* (Cork, 1967); (2) *Non-fiction* (Cork, 1969); (3) *Irish* (Cork, 1971).
Rann. No. 20 (June 1953). Belfast.
This magazine has several valuable articles on writing in Ulster as well as a useful bio-bibliographical list of Ulster authors, 1900-53.
S. H. Bell, N. A. Robb and John Hewitt (ed.). *The arts in Ulster, a symposium.* London, 1951.
S. H. Bell. *The theatre in Ulster.* Dublin, 1972.
Irish Booklore. Belfast, 1971-

OLD PHOTOGRAPHS
Maurice Gorham. *Ireland from old photographs.* London, 1971.
Theodora Fitzgibbon. *Taste of Ireland: Irish traditional food,* (illustrated). London, 1968.
Noel Nesbit. *The changing face of Belfast.* Belfast, 1968.
Kieran Hickey. *The light of other days: Irish life at the turn of the century in the photographs of Robert French.* London, 1973.

INDEX OF AUTHORS

Legananny dolmen, near Castle-wellan, Co. Down (Linenhall Library)

LEA

ACKNOWLEDGEMENTS

For kind permission to reprint copywright material, the following acknowledgements are made:- For a poem by Sir Shane Leslie to Desmond Leslie. For a poem by Moira O'Neill to Mrs. Susan Skrine. For a poem by Alice Milligan to Gill and MacMillan Ltd. For a poem by Patrick MacGill to T.C. Johnson. For a poem by Joseph Campbell to Simon Campbell. For a poem by Enrí Ó'Muirgheasa to Miss Maeve Ó'Muirgheasa. For an extract from George Birmingham to Irish University Press. For an extract from Lynn Doyle to Mrs. Jonathan Fisher. For an extract from Stephen Gwynn to Blackie & Son Ltd. For an extract from A.McK. Ros to her literary executors and Chatto and Windus Ltd. For an extract from F.F. Moore to Hutchinson Publishing Group Ltd. For an extract from G.W. Russell to his literary executors. For an extract from Robert Lynd to Mills and Boon Ltd. For an extract from Rutherford Mayne to Miss Ginette Waddell. For an extract from M.E. Dobbs from Brigadier N.C. Dobbs. For an extract from L.J. Walsh to his literary executors. For an extract from Forrest Reid to Stephen Gilbert. For an extract from St. J. Ervine to his literary executors.

For kind permission to use photographs the following acknowledgements are made:- For photographs from the Cooper Collection to H.D.H. Cooper. For photographs from the Rose Shaw Collection to Peter Verschoyle. For photographs from the Green Collection to the trustees of the Ulster Folk and Transport Museum. For photographs from the Lawrence Collection to the director of the National Library of Ireland. For photographs from the Sprott Collection to the headmaster of Portadown College. For photographs from the Welch and Hogg Collections to the trustees of the Ulster Museum. For photographs from the Public Record Office to the deputy-keeper. For photographs from the Royal Irish Academy to the officers of the Academy. For photographs from the Linenhall Library to the governors of the Library. For photographs from private collections to S.H. Bell, Stephen Gilbert, J.K.C. Armour and Fred Heatley.

Every effort has been made to trace the owners of copyright material used in this book. In the event of omission the publisher would be glad of notification.